SCIENTISTS. Their Lives and Works

ISSN: 1522-8630

SCIENTISTS: Their Lives and Works

Marie C. Ellavich

VOLUME 6

U·X·L®
AN IMPRINT OF THE GALE GROUP

DETROIT • LONDON

Scientists: Their Lives and Works

Volume 6

Marie C. Ellavich

Staff

Elizabeth Des Chenes, *U·X·L Senior Editor*
Carol DeKane Nagel, *U·X·L Managing Editor*
Thomas L. Romig, *U·X·L Publisher*

Keasha Jack-Lyles, *Permission Associate* (Pictures)

Deborah Milliken, *Production Assistant*
Evi Seoud, *Assistant Production Manager*
Mary Beth Trimper, *Production Director*

Pamela A. E. Galbreath, *Senior Art Director*
Cynthia Baldwin, *Product Design Manager*
Barbara J. Yarrow, *Graphic Services Manager*
Linda Mahoney, LM Design, *Typesetting*

ISBN 0-7876-3682-7

ISSN 1522–8630

Front cover photographs were received from the following sources (clockwise from top right): Luis Alvarez, Robert H. Goddard (reproduced by permission of AP/Wide World Photos); Margaret Mead (reproduced by permission of the Bettmann Archive). Back cover photographs were received from the following sources (top to bottom): Edwin H. Land (reproduced by permission of AP/Wide World Photos); George Washington Carver (reproduced by permission of the Bettmann Archive).

Printed in the United States of America

10 9 8 7 6 5 4 3 2 1

Contents

Nettie Maria Stevens.
Reproduced by permission
of the Science
Photo Library/Photo
Researchers, Inc.

Scientists by Field of Specialization

Includes *Scientists*, volumes 1-6.
Italic type indicates volume numbers.

*Howard Aiken.
Reproduced by permission
of Corbis-Bettmann.*

Ecology

Electrical Engineering

Engineering

Entomology

Environmentalism

Industrial Medicine

Invention

Physical Chemistry

Physics

Physiology

Primatology

Psychiatry

Psychology

Reader's Guide

B udding scientists and those entering the fascinating world of science for fun or study will find inspiration in this sixth volume of *Scientists*. The series presents detailed biographies of the women and men whose theories, discoveries, and inventions have revolutionized science and society. From Ptolemy to Bill Gates and George Washington Carver to Margaret Mead, *Scientists* explores the pioneers and their innovations that students most want to learn about.

Scientists from around the world and from all time periods are featured, in fields such as astronomy, ecology, oceanography, physics, and more.

In *Scientists,* volume 6, students will find:

• Thirty-four scientist biographies, each focusing on the scientist's early life, formative experiences, and inspirations—details that keep students reading

• "Impact" boxes that draw out important information and sum up why each scientist's work is indeed revolutionary

Hypatia of Alexandria. Reproduced by permission of Corbis-Bettmann.

• Thirty-five boxes that highlight individuals who influenced the work of the featured scientist or who conducted similar research, as well as related information of special interest to students

• Sources for further reading so students know where to delve even deeper

• More than forty black-and-white portraits and additional photographs that give students a better understanding of the people and inventions discussed

Scientists, volume 6, includes a list of the scientists in all six volumes, categorized by fields ranging from aeronautical engineering to zoology; a timeline of major scientific breakthroughs; and a glossary of scientific terms used in the text. Cross references direct the student to related entries throughout the six-volume set. The volume concludes with a cumulative subject index for the series so that students can easily find the people, inventions, and theories discussed throughout *Scientists.*

Suggestions

We welcome any comments on this work and suggestions for individuals to feature in future editions of *Scientists.* Please write: Editors, *Scientists,* U•X•L, 27500 Drake Rd., Farmington Hills, MI 48331–3535; call toll-free: 1–800–877–4253; or fax: 1–800–414–5043.

Timeline of Scientific Breakthroughs

335 B.C. Greek philosopher and scientist **Aristotle** founds the Lyceum and lays the foundation for centuries of Western thought.

A.D.100–170 During his lifetime, Egyptian astronomer **Ptolemy** popularizes the geocentric theory of the universe.

A.D. 400 **Hypatia,** the only famous female scholar of ancient times, becomes the director of the Neoplatonic School in Alexandria, Egypt.

1577 Danish astronomer **Tycho Brahe** disproves the ancient idea of physical structures holding up the planets after he observes the movement of a comet.

Robert C. Gallo.
Reproduced by permission
of Archive Photos, Inc.

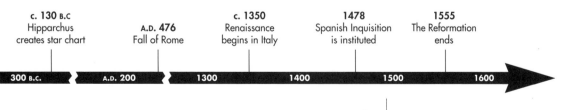

c. 130 B.C
Hipparchus
creates star chart

A.D. 476
Fall of Rome

c. 1350
Renaissance
begins in Italy

1478
Spanish Inquisition
is instituted

1555
The Reformation
ends

| 300 B.C. | A.D. 200 | 1300 | 1400 | 1500 | 1600 |

1673	German mathematician **Gottfried Wilhelm Leibniz** creates integral and differential calculus.
1752	American inventor **Benjamin Franklin** performs his famous kite experiment, proving that thunderstorms contain an electrical charge.
1870s	Russian mathematician **Sonya Vasilyevna Kovalevsky** develops an important mathematical theory later known as the Cauchy-Kovalevsky theorem.
1892	American forester **Gifford Pinchot** establishes the scientific study and practice of forestry in the United States.
1902	American physician **Walter Reed** helps discover that the deadly disease yellow fever is carried by mosquitoes.
1903	American biologist **Nettie Maria Stevens** begins her research career, during which she makes important discoveries about chromosomes.
1904	The first African American psychiatrist, **Solomon Fuller,** begins studying both the physical and psychological symptoms of his patients.
1906	Canadian-born American botanist **Alice Eastwood** rebuilds a valuable plant collection after a major earthquake and fire in San Francisco, California.
1910	American geneticist **Thomas Hunt Morgan** lays the groundwork for the modern field of genetics after experimenting with fruit flies.
1918	American bacteriologist **Rebecca Craighill Lancefield** begins studying streptococcus bacteria, and eventually develops a system to classify the bacteria.

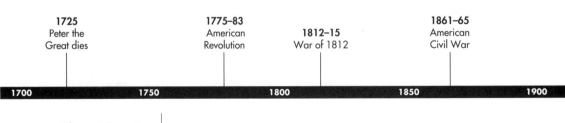

1725
Peter the
Great dies

1775–83
American
Revolution

1812–15
War of 1812

1861–65
American
Civil War

1700	1750	1800	1850	1900

1923   Indian physicist **Satyendranath Bose** develops an important proof that supports Albert Einstein's ideas about the behavior of protons.

1927   English zoologist **Charles Elton** publishes *Animal Ecology* and helps establish animal ecology as a distinct field of scientific study.

1927   Belgian mathematical physicist **Georges Lemaître** publishes his big bang theory of the creation of the universe.

1936   Danish geophysicist **Inge Lehmann** discovers that there is a solid core at the center of the earth.

1937   Pioneering female Canadian aeronautical engineer **Elsie Gregory MacGill** begins building the Maple Leaf Trainer II.

1937   American ornithologist **Margaret Morse Nice** publishes the first part of her landmark work on bird behavior, *Studies in the Life History of the Song Sparrow.*

1939   Hungarian-born physicist **Leo Szilard** devises the concept of nuclear fission which is used to create the first atomic bombs.

1939   American microbiologist and pediatrician **Hattie Alexander** develops a successful treatment for influenzal meningitis, a deadly childhood disease.

1940   American pathologist **Harriet Hardy** begins investigating industrial illnesses such as berylliosis.

1940   American zoologist **Libbie Henrietta Hyman** publishes *The Invertebrates.*

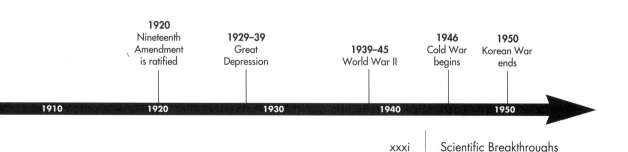

1920
Nineteenth
Amendment
is ratified

1929–39
Great
Depression

1939–45
World War II

1946
Cold War
begins

1950
Korean War
ends

1910   1920   1930   1940   1950

   Scientific Breakthroughs

1943   American computer engineer **Howard Aiken** completes work on the world's first large-scale digital computer, the Mark I.

1953   Developed from the research of Russian physicists **Andrei Sakharov** and Igor Tamm, the first Soviet hydrogen bomb is field-tested.

1955   American paleoecologist **Estella Bergere Leopold** begins her career, during which she becomes a leading authority on prehistoric organisms and environments.

1965   Leading English mathematician and physicist **Roger Penrose** helps to determine the existence of black holes.

1967   Argentinean heart surgeon **René Geronimo Favaloro** pioneers the use of heart bypass surgery as a standard surgical procedure.

1974   Mexican atmospheric chemist **Mario Molina** reports that chloroflourocarbons, or CFCs, are a major factor in the destruction of the ozone layer.

1984   American medical researcher **Robert C. Gallo** proves that HIV causes AIDS.

1987   Chinese physicist **Paul Ching-Wu Chu** discovers new superconducting materials.

1993   American medical researcher **Nancy Wexler** discovers the cause of Huntington's Disease.

1997   American chemical researcher **Karen Wetterhahn** dies of mercury poisoning as a result of conducting an experiment to help the environment.

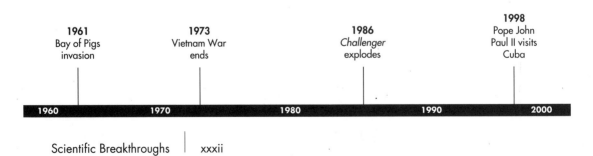

1961
Bay of Pigs
invasion

1973
Vietnam War
ends

1986
Challenger
explodes

1998
Pope John
Paul II visits
Cuba

| 1960 | 1970 | 1980 | 1990 | 2000 |

Words to Know

A

Absolute zero: the theoretical point at which a substance has no heat and motion ceases; equivalent to -276°C or -459.67°F.

Algae: a diverse group of plant or plantlike organisms that grow mainly in water.

Alpha particle: a positively charged nuclear particle that consists of two protons and two electrons; it is ejected at a high speed from disintegrating radioactive materials.

Alternating current: the flow of electrons first in one direction and then in the other at regular intervals.

Amino acids: organic acids that are the chief components of proteins.

Anatomy: the study of the structure and form of biological organisms.

Anthropology: the science that deals with the study of human beings, especially their origin, development, divisions, and customs.

Aorta: the main artery of the human body that starts out at the left ventricle of the heart and carries blood to all organs except the heart.

Archaeology: the scientific study of material remains, such as fossils and relics, of past societies.

Artificial intelligence: the branch of science concerned with the development of machines having the ability to perform tasks normally thought to require human intelligence, such as problem solving, discriminating among single objects, and response to spoken commands.

Asteroid: one of thousands of small planets located in a belt between the orbits of Mars and Jupiter.

Astronomy: the study of the physical and chemical properties of objects and matter outside Earth's atmosphere.

Astrophysics: the branch of physics involving the study of the physical and chemical nature of celestial objects and events.

Atomic bomb: a weapon of mass destruction that derives its explosive energy from nuclear fission.

Atomic weight: the mass of one atom of an element.

B

Bacteria: a large, diverse group of mostly single-celled organisms that play a key role in the decay of organic matter and the cycling of nutrients.

Bacteriology: the scientific study of bacteria, their characteristics, and their activities as related to medicine, industry, and agriculture.

Bacteriophage: a virus that infects bacteria.

Ballistic missile: a self-propelled object (like a rocket) that is guided as it ascends into the air and usually falls freely.

Behaviorism: the school of psychology that holds that human and animal behavior is based not on independent will nor motivation but rather on response to reward and punishment.

Beta decay: process by which a neutron in an atomic nucleus breaks apart into a proton and an electron.

Big bang: in astronomy, the theory that the universe resulted from a cosmic explosion that occurred billions of years ago and then expanded over time.

Binary stars: a system of two stars revolving around each other under a mutual gravitation system.

Binary system: a system that uses the numbers 1 and 0 to correspond to the on or off states of electric current.

Biochemistry: the study of chemical compounds and processes occurring in living organisms.

Biodiversity: the number of different species of plants and animals in a specified region.

Biofeedback: a method of learning to gain some voluntary control over involuntary bodily functions like heartbeat or blood pressure.

Biology: the scientific study of living organisms.

Biophysics: the branch of biology in which the methods and principles of physics are applied to the study of living things.

Biosynthesis: the creation of a chemical compound in the body.

Biotechnology: use of biological organisms, systems, or processes to make or modify products.

Black holes: regions in space that exert an extremely intense gravitational force from which nothing, including light, can escape.

Botany: the branch of biology involving the study of plant life.

Byte: a group of binary digits (0 and 1) that a computer processes as a unit.

C

Carbon filament: a threadlike object in a lamp that glows when electricity passes through it.

Carburetor: the device that supplies an internal-combustion engine with a mixture of vaporized fuel and air that, when ignited, produces the engine's energy.

Carcinogen: a cancer-causing agent, such as a chemical or a virus.

Catalyst: a substance that enables a chemical reaction to take place either more quickly or under otherwise difficult conditions.

Cathode: a negatively charged electrode.

Cathode rays: electrons emitted by a cathode when heated.

Cerebrum: the uppermost part of the brain that, in higher mammals, covers the rest of the brain and is considered to be the seat of conscious mental processes.

Chemistry: the science of the nature, composition, and properties of material substances and their transformations.

Chromosome: threadlike structure in the nucleus of a cell that carries thousands of genes.

Circuit: the complete path of an electric current including the source of electric energy; an assemblage of electronic elements.

Classification: a system of naming and categorizing plants and animals in which they are grouped by the number of physical traits they have in common. The ranking system goes from general to specific: kingdom, phylum, class, order, family, genus, and species.

Climatology: the scientific study of climates and their phenomena.

Combustion: a rapid chemical process that produces heat and light.

Conductor: a substance able to carry an electrical current.

Conservation biology: the branch of biology that involves conserving rapidly vanishing wild animals, plants, and places.

Conservation laws: laws of physics that state that a particular property, mass, energy, momentum, or electrical charge is not lost during any change.

Cosmic rays: charged particles, mainly the nuclei of hydrogen and other atoms, that bombard Earth's upper atmosphere at velocities close to that of light.

Cosmology: the study of the structure and evolution of the universe.

Cross-fertilization: a method of fertilization in which the gametes (mature male or female cells) are produced by separate individuals or sometimes by individuals of different kinds.

Cryogenics: the branch of physics that involves the production and effects of very low temperatures.

Crystallography: the science that deals with the forms and structures of crystals.

Cytology: the branch of biology concerned with the study of cells.

D

Deforestation: the process of cutting down all the trees in a forest.

Desertification: the changing of productive land to desert, often by clearing the land of trees and other plant life.

Diffraction: the spreading and bending of light waves as they pass through a hole or slit.

Direct current: a regular flow of electrons, always in the same direction.

DNA (deoxyribonucleic acid): a long molecule composed of two chains of nucleotides (organic chemicals) that contain the genetic information carried from one generation to another.

E

Earthquake: an unpredictable event in which masses of rock shift below Earth's surface, releasing enormous amounts of energy and sending out shockwaves that sometimes cause the ground to shake dramatically.

Ecology: the branch of science dealing with the interrelationship of organisms and their environments.

Ecosystem: community of plants and animals and the physical environment with which they interact.

Electrocardiograph: an instrument that makes a graphic record of the heart's movements.

Electrochemistry: the branch of physical chemistry involving the relation of electricity to chemical changes.

Electrodes: conductors used to establish electrical contact with a nonmetallic part of a circuit.

Electromagnetism: the study of electric and magnetic fields and their interaction with electric charges and currents.

Electron: a negatively charged particle that orbits the nucleus of an atom.

Embryo: an animal in the early stages of development before birth.

Embryology: the study of embryos and their development.

Entomology: the branch of zoology dealing with the study of insects.

Environmentalism: the movement to preserve and improve the natural environment, and particularly to control pollution.

Enzyme: any of numerous complex proteins that are produced by living cells and spark specific biochemical reactions.

Epidemiology: the study of the causes, distribution, and control of disease in populations.

Equinox: the two times each year when the Sun crosses the plane of Earth's equator; at these times, day and night are of equal length everywhere on Earth.

Ethnobotany: the plant lore of a race of people.

Ethnology: science that deals with the division of human beings into races and their origin, distribution, relations, and characteristics.

Ethology: the scientific and objective study of the behavior of animals in the wild rather than in captivity.

Evolution: in the struggle for survival, the process by which successive generations of a species pass on to their offspring the characteristics that enable the species to survive.

Extinction: the total disappearance of a species or the disappearance of a species from a given area.

F

Flora: the plants of a particular region or environment.

Foramen magnum: the opening at the base of the skull through which the spinal cord enters the cranial cavity.

Fossils: the remains, traces, or impressions of living organisms that inhabited Earth more than ten thousand years ago.

Frontal systems: a weather term denoting the boundaries between air masses of different temperatures and humidities.

G

Gamma rays: short electromagnetic wavelengths that come from the nuclei of atoms during radioactive decay.

Game theory: the mathematics involved in determining the effect of a particular strategy in a competition, as in a game of chess, a military battle, or in selling products.

Gene: in classical genetics, a unit of hereditary information that is carried on chromosomes and determines observable characteristics; in molecular genetics, a special sequence of DNA or RNA located on the chromosome.

Genetic code: the means by which genetic information is translated into the chromosomes that make up living organisms.

Genetics: the study of inheritance in living organisms.

Genome: genetic material of a human being; the complete genetic structure of a species.

Geochemistry: the study of the chemistry of Earth (and other planets).

Geology: the study of the origin, history, and structure of Earth.

Geophysics: the physics of Earth, including studies of the atmosphere, earthquakes, volcanism, and oceans.

Global warming: the rise in Earth's temperature that is attributed to the buildup of carbon dioxide and other pollutants in the atmosphere.

Gravity: the force of attraction (causing free objects to accelerate toward each other) that exists between the surface of Earth (as well as other planets) and bodies at or near its surface.

Greenhouse effect: warming of Earth's atmosphere due to the absorption of heat by molecules of water vapor, carbon dioxide, methane, ozone, nitrous oxide, and chlorofluorocarbons.

H

Heliocentric: having the Sun as the center.

Herpetology: the branch of zoology that deals with reptiles and amphibians.

Histology: the study of microscopic plant and animal tissues.

Hominids: humanlike creatures.

Hormones: chemical messengers produced in living organisms that play significant roles in the body, such as affecting growth, metabolism, and digestion.

Horticulture: the science of growing fruits, vegetables, and ornamental plants.

Hybridization: cross-pollination of plants of different varieties to produce seed.

Hydraulics: the study of the forces of fluids as they apply to accomplishing mechanical or practical tasks.

Hydrodynamics: the study of the forces exerted by fluids in motion.

Hydrostatics: a branch of physics that studies fluids at rest and the forces they exert, particularly on submerged objects.

Hypothesis: an assumption made on the basis of scientific data that is an attempt to explain a principle in nature but remains tentative because of lack of solid evidence.

I

Immunology: the branch of medicine concerned with the body's ability to protect itself from disease.

Imprinting: the rapid learning process that takes place early in the life of a social animal and establishes a behavioral pattern, such as a recognition of and attraction to its own kind or a substitute.

In vitro fertilization: fertilization of eggs outside of the body.

Infrared radiation: electromagnetic rays released by hot objects; also known as a heat radiation.

Infertility: the inability to produce offspring for any reason.

Internal-combustion engine: an engine in which the combustion (burning) that generates the heat that powers it goes on inside the engine itself, rather than in a furnace.

Invertebrates: animals lacking a spinal column.

Ion: an atom or groups of atoms that carries an electrical charge—either positive or negative—as a result of losing or gaining one or more electrons.

Isomers: compound that have the same number of atoms of the same elements, but different properties because their atoms are arranged differently.

Isotope: one of two or more atoms of a chemical element that have the same structure but different physical properties.

L

Laser: acronym for light amplification by stimulated emission of radiation; a device that produces intense light with a precisely defined wavelength.

Light-year: in astronomy, the distance light travels in one year, about six trillion miles.

Limnology: the branch of biology concerning freshwater plants.

Logic: the science of the formal principles of reasoning.

Lunar eclipse: the passing of the Moon either wholly or partially into the shadow created by Earth's position in front of the Sun; that is, when the three bodies align thus: Moon—Earth—Sun.

M

Magnetic field: the space around an electric current or a magnet in which a magnetic force can be observed.

Maser: acronym for microwave amplification of stimulated emission of radiation; a device that produces radiation in short wavelengths.

Metabolism: the process by which living cells break down organic compounds to produce energy.

Metallurgy: the science and technology of metals.

Meteorology: the science that deals with the atmosphere and its phenomena and with weather and weather forecasting.

Microbiology: branch of biology dealing with microscopic forms of life.

Microwaves: electromagnetic radiation waves between one millimeter and one centimeter in length.

Molecular biology: the study of the structure and function of molecules that make up living organisms.

Molecule: the smallest particle of a substance that retains all the properties of the substance and is composed of one or more atoms.

Moving assembly line: a system in a plant or factory in which an item that is being made is carried past a series of workers who remain in their places. Each worker assembles a particular portion of the finished product and then repeats the same process with the next item.

Mutation: any permanent change in hereditary material, involving either a physical change in chromosome relations or a biochemical change in genes.

N

Natural selection: the natural process by which groups best adjusted to their environment survive and reproduce, thereby passing on to their offspring genetic qualities best suited to that environment.

Nebulae: large, cloudy bodies of dust in space.

Nerve Growth Factor (NGF): the nutrients that determine how nerve cells take on their specific roles in the nervous system.

Nervous system: the bodily system that in vertebrates is made up of the brain and spinal cord, nerves, ganglia, and other organs and that receives and interprets stimuli and transmits impulses to targeted organs.

Neurology: the scientific study of the nervous system, especially its structure, functions, and abnormalities.

Neurosecretion: the process of producing a secretion by nerve cells.

Neurosurgery: surgery on the nerves, brain, or spinal cord.

Neurosis: any emotional or mental disorder that affects only part of the personality, such as anxiety or mild depression, as a result of stress.

Neutron: an uncharged particle found in atomic nuclei.

Neutron star: a hypothetical dense celestial object that consists primarily of closely packed neutrons that results from the collapse of a much larger celestial body.

Nova: a star that suddenly increases in light output and then fades away to its former obscure state within a few months or years.

Nuclear fallout: the drifting of radioactive particles into the atmosphere as the result of nuclear explosions.

Nuclear fission: the process in which an atomic nucleus is split, resulting in the release of large amounts of energy.

Nuclear physics: physics that deals with the atomic nucleus, atomic energy, the atom bomb, or atomic power.

Nucleotides: compounds that form the basic stuctural units—the stairs on the spiral staircase—of DNA, and are arranged on the staircase in a pattern of heredity-carrying code "words."

Nutritionist: a person who studies the ways in which living organisms take in and make use of food.

O

Oceanography: the science that deals with the study of oceans and seas.

Optics: the study of light and vision.

Organic: of, relating to, or arising in a bodily organ

Ornithology: the study of birds.

Ozone layer: the atmospheric layer of approximately twenty to thirty miles above Earth's surface that protects the lower atmosphere from harmful solar radiation.

P

Paleoanthropology: the branch of anthropology dealing with the study of mammal fossils.

Paleoecology: the study of prehistoric organisms and their environments.

Paleontology: the study of the life of past geological periods as known from fossil remains.

Particle physics: the branch of physics concerned with the study of the constitution, properties, and interactions of elementary particles.

Particles: the smallest building blocks of energy and matter.

Patent: a government grant giving an inventor the right to be the only person to sell an invention for a set length of time.

Pathology: the study of the essential nature of diseases, especially the structural and functional changes produced by them.

Pediatrics: a branch of medicine involving the development, care, and diseases of children.

Pendulum: an object that hangs freely from a fixed point and swings back and forth under the action of gravity; often used to regulate movement, as the pendulum in a clock.

Periodic table: a table of the elements in order of atomic number, arranged in rows and columns to show periodic similarities and trends in physical and chemical properties.

Pharmacology: the science dealing with the properties, reactions, and therapeutic values of drugs.

Phylum: the first division of the animal kingdom in the Linnaeus classification system. The ranking of the system is in order from the general to the specific—kingdom, phylum, class, order, family, genus, and species.

Physics: the science that explores the physical properties and composition of objects and the forces that affect them.

Physiology: the branch of biology that deals with the functions and actions of life or of living matter, such as organs, tissues, and cells.

Planetologist: a person who studies the physical bodies in the solar system, including planets and their satellites, comets, and meteorites.

Plankton: floating animal and plant life.

Plasma physics: the branch of physics involving the study of electrically charged, extremely hot gases.

Primate: any order of mammals composed of humans, apes, or monkeys.

Projectile motion: the movement of an object thrust forward by an external force—for example, a cannonball shot out of a cannon.

Protein: large molecules found in all living organisms that are essential to the structure and functioning of all living cells.

Proton: a positively charged particle found in atomic nuclei.

Psychiatry: the branch of medicine that deals with mental, emotional, and behavioral disorders.

Psychoanalysis: the method of analyzing psychic phenomenon and treating emotional disorders that involves treatment sessions during which the patient is encouraged to talk freely about personal experiences, especially about early childhood and dreams.

Psychophysiology: a branch of psychology that focuses on combined mental and bodily processes.

Psychology: the study of human and animal behavior.

Psychotic: a person with severe emotional or mental disorders that cause a loss of contact with reality.

Q

Quantum: any of the very small increments or parcels into which many forms of energy are subdivided.

Quasar: celestial object more distant than stars that emits excessive amounts of radiation.

R

Radar: acronym for radio detection and ranging; the process of using radio waves to detect objects.

Radiation: energy emitted in the form of waves or particles.

Radio waves: electromagnetic radiation.

Radioactive fallout: the radioactive particles resulting from a nuclear explosion.

Radioactivity: the property possessed by some elements (as uranium) or isotopes (as carbon 14) of spontaneously emitting energetic particles (as electrons or alpha particles) by disintegration of their atomic nuclei.

Radiology: the branch of medicine that uses X rays and radium (an intensely radioactive metallic element) to diagnose and treat disease.

Redshift: the increase in the wavelength of all light received from a celestial object (or wave source), usually because the object is moving away from the observer.

RNA (ribonucleic acid): any of various nucleic acids that are associated with the control of cellular chemical activities.

S

Scientific method: collecting evidence meticulously and theorizing from it.

Seismograph: a device that records vibrations of the ground and within Earth.

Seismology: the study and measurement of earthquakes.

Semiconductor: substances whose ability to carry electrical current is lower than that of a conductor (like metal) and higher than that of insulators (like rubber).

Shortwave: a radio wave having a wavelength between ten and one hundred meters.

Slide rule: a calculating device that, in its simplest form, consists of a ruler and a sliding attachment that are graduated with logarithm tables.

Social science: the study of human society and individual relationships within it, including the fields of sociology, anthropology, economics, political sicence, and history.

Sociobiology: the systematic study of the biological basis for all social behavior.

Soil erosion: the loss of usable topsoil, often due to clearing trees and other plant life from the land.

Solid state: using semiconductor devices rather than electron tubes.

Spectrum: the range of colors produced by individual elements within a light source.

Statics: a branch of physics that explores the forces of equilibrium, or balance.

Steady-state theory: a theory that proposes that the universe has neither a beginning nor an end.

Stellar spectra: the distinctive mix of radiation emitted by every star.

Stellar spectroscopy: the process that breaks a star's light into component colors so that the various elements of the star can be observed.

Sterilization: boiling or heating of instruments and food to prevent proliferation of microorganisms.

Supernova: a catastrophic explosion in which a large portion of a star's mass is blown out into space, or the star is entirely destroyed.

T

Theorem: in mathematics, a formula, proposition, or statement.

Theory: an assumption drawn from scientific evidence that provides a plausible explanation for the principle or principles behind a natural phenomenon. (A *theory* generally has more evidence behind it and finds more acceptance in the scientific community than a *hypothesis*.)

Thermodynamics: the branch of physics that deals with the mechanical action or relations of heat.

Trace element: a chemical element present in minute quantities.

Transistor: a solid-state electronic device that is used to control the flow of electricity in electronic equipment and consists of a small block of semiconductor with at least three electrodes.

V

Vaccine: a preparation administered to increase immunity to polio.

Vacuum tube: an electric tube from which all matter has been removed.

Variable stars: stars whose light output varies because of internal fluctuations or because they are eclipsed by another star.

Variation: in genetics, differences in traits of a particular species.

Vertebrate: an animal that has a spinal column.

Virology: the study of viruses.

Virtual reality: an artificial computer-created environment that seeks to mimic reality.

Virus: a microscopic agent of infection.

Voltaic pile: a basic form of battery that was the first source of continuous and controllable electric current.

W

Wavelength: the distance between one peak of a wave of light, heat, or energy and the next corresponding peak.

X

X ray: a form of electromagnetic radiation with an extremely short wavelength that is produced by bombarding a metallic target with electrons in a vacuum.

Z

Zoology: the branch of biology concerned with the study of animal life.

Zooplankton: small drifting animal life in the ocean.

SCIENTISTS: Their Lives and Works

Howard Aiken

Born March 8, 1900
Hoboken, New Jersey
Died March 14, 1973

Noted physicist and Harvard professor Howard Aiken designed and built the Mark I computer in the late 1930s and early 1940s. The Mark I was the first large-scale digital computer (a computer that operates with numbers expressed directly as digits), and it became the inspiration for larger and more advanced computing machines. Each of Aiken's later creations—the Mark II, Mark III, and Mark IV—reached a new level in speed and calculating capacity.

Howard Aiken built the Mark I, the first large-scale digital computer.

Difficult student days

Howard Hathaway Aiken was born on March 8, 1900, in Hoboken, New Jersey, and grew up in Indianapolis, Indiana. Because his family was not wealthy, Aiken had to take a job when he completed the eighth grade. He worked twelve-hour shifts seven nights a week as a switchboard operator for the Indianapolis Light and Heat Company. During the day he attended Arsenal Technical High School. When the school

1

Computer engineer Howard Aiken developed the Mark I, the world's first large-scale digital computer. Ultimately he produced a series of four Mark computer models, each of which was capable of increasingly greater speed and computing capacity. Simple computers had been developed before Aiken's Mark machines, but these early models used punched card commands. Aiken's machines were a major innovation because they automated the method of providing a computer with information. By the time the Mark III was built, Aiken had incorporated an electronic memory system into his computer. This achievement paved the way for even faster and more powerful computers in the years to come.

superintendent learned of Aiken's round-the-clock work and study schedule, he arranged a series of special tests that allowed the young man to graduate early.

Begins Harvard career

In 1919 Aiken entered the University of Wisconsin at Madison. He also worked part-time for the local gas company. After receiving a bachelor of science degree in 1923, he was immediately promoted to chief engineer at the gas company. Over the next twelve years Aiken became a professor at the University of Miami in Florida and then went into business for himself. By 1935, however, he had decided he wanted to return to school to work on a Ph.D. He began graduate studies at the University of Chicago in Illinois before going on to Harvard University in Cambridge, Massachusetts. Upon earning a master's degree in physics in 1937, Aiken became an instructor at Harvard. Two years later he received his doctorate. In 1941 Aiken was appointed associate professor of applied mathematics and promoted to full professor in 1946.

Proposes first modern computer

While Aiken was completing his graduate work in physics, he had to spend many hours on long and tedious calculations. This experience prompted him to think seriously about improving calculating machines (devices for performing mathematical calculations) in order to reduce the time needed for figuring large numerical sequences. In 1937, when Aiken began teaching at Harvard, he wrote a twenty-two-page memo proposing an initial design for a new machine. Aiken's idea was to build a computer with electromagnetic (magnetism from electricity) components that would be controlled by coded sequences of instructions. His computer would run by itself after a particular process had been developed. At that time calculators used punched cards (small pieces of cardboard with patterned holes), which could carry out only one arithmetic operation at a time.

Aiken proposed that these machines could be modified to become fully automated and perform a wide range of arithmetic and mathematical functions. His original design was inspired by a calculator invented by the nineteenth-century English mathematician Charles Babbage (see entry in volume one). Babbage had devoted nearly forty years to developing a calculating machine, which was never fully implemented.

Finds support for Mark I

Harvard offered little support for Aiken's idea, so he turned to private industry for assistance. After consulting several companies, Aiken finally approached International Business Machines (IBM). At the time, IBM manufactured office machines only, but company executives wanted to encourage research in new and promising areas. IBM officials were so impressed with Aiken's idea that the company agreed to finance the construction of the Mark I computer with additional funding from the U.S. Navy. The navy supported Aiken's computer because the Mark I could potentially speed up the complex mathematical calculations involved in aiming long-range guns on warships. For instance, the Mark I could calculate gun trajectories (shooting paths) in a matter of minutes.

Mark I debuts

Having secured assistance for building the Mark I, Aiken began work at IBM laboratories in Endicott, New York. His machine was electromechanical (a mechanical device controlled by electricity) and used ordinary telephone relays (switches activated by electricity) that allowed electrical cur-

Punched Card Precedes Floppy Disk

In the 1940s computer engineer Howard Aiken had to rely upon technology that was crude by today's standards. Now that computers can be found in almost every household, accessories such as the floppy disk have become common. When Aiken began developing his Mark I computer, however, he did not have floppy disks for feeding data into the machine. Instead, he had to use a punched card. Invented in 1801 by Joseph Marie Jacquard (1752–1834), the punched card was later adopted by Herman Hollerith (1860–1929) for use in tabulating machines. Hollerith built a machine that compiled information from the 1890 U.S. Census in only six weeks. The punched card survived until it was replaced by the more efficient floppy disk.

rents to be switched on or off. The computer consisted of thousands of relays and other components, all assembled in a stainless steel and glass frame that was fifty-one feet long and eight feet high. The Mark I was completed in 1943 and installed at Harvard a year later. The heart of the machine was formed by seventy-two rotating registers (devices for storing data), each of which could store a twenty-three-digit positive or negative number. The telephone relays established communication between the registers. Instructions and data were entered into the computer by means of continuous strips of punched paper, then printed by two electrical typewriters hooked up to the machine.

Continues to improve computer

The Mark I did not resemble modern computers, either in appearance or in principles of operation. For instance, the machine had no keyboard (a systematically arranged set of keys by which a device is operated). Instead, it was operated with approximately 1,400 rotary switches that had to be adjusted each time data was entered. Although clumsy by today's standards, the Mark I was a major improvement over earlier machines because it was much faster. Scientists and engineers were eager to use the Mark I, thus proving the project's success and giving Aiken the added inspiration for work on improved models. However, a dispute developed with IBM over credit for the Mark I, and the company eventually withdrew support for all of Aiken's further efforts. Despite these problems, Aiken began working on a more powerful model in response to competition from the ENIAC, a computer then being built at Columbia University in New York City.

Uses electronic components

Aiken went on to produce three other models—the Mark II, Mark III, and Mark IV. With the Mark III, he began building machines that used electronic components. Originally, Aiken had taken a conservative view of electronic engineering, which led him to sacrifice the speed offered by electronic technology for the dependability of electromechanical components. Then, following World War II (1939–1945), he began to feel comfortable using electronics. In 1949 Aiken completed the Mark III, which was composed mainly of electronic components. Data and instructions were stored on magnetic drums with a capacity of 4,350 sixteen-bit words and roughly 4,000 instructions. (A bit is a unit of computer information.) Nevertheless, the final version of the Mark III still contained about two thousand mechanical relays in addition to its electronic components. The Mark IV, however, was considerably faster.

Advances computer technology

Aiken's work made a significant contribution to early computing technology. His machines demonstrated that a large, calculating computer could not only be built but could also provide the scientific world with high-powered, speedy mathematical solutions to a wide range of problems. Aiken remained at Harvard until 1961, when he moved back to Florida. He was appointed Distinguished Professor of Information at the University of Miami, where he established a computer science program and a computing center. At that time he also founded a consulting firm, Howard Aiken Industries Incorporated, in New York. Aiken disliked the idea of patents and was known for sharing his work with others. He died on March 14, 1973.

Further Reading

Augarten, Stan, *Bit by Bit,* Ticknor & Fields, 1984.

Fang, Irving E., *The Computer Story,* Rada Press, 1988.

Moreau, R., *The Computer Comes of Age,* MIT Press, 1984.

Ritchie, David, *The Computer Pioneers: The Making of the Modern Computer,* Simon and Schuster, 1986.

Slater, Robert, *Portraits in Silicon,* MIT Press, 1987.

Stine, Harry G., *The Untold Story of the Computer Revolution: Bits, Bytes, Bauds, and Brains,* Arbor House, 1985.

Wulforst, Harry, *Breakthrough to the Computer Age,* Scribner's, 1982.

Hattie Alexander

Born April 5, 1901
Baltimore, Maryland
Died June 24, 1968

Hattie Elizabeth Alexander was a dedicated pediatrician (children's doctor), medical educator, and researcher in microbiology (a branch of biology dealing with microscopic forms of life). Alexander won international recognition for discovering a serum (the liquid part of blood, which contains disease-fighting antibodies) to combat influenzal meningitis, a childhood disease that at one time was nearly always fatal. Alexander also investigated microbiological genetics (a branch of research that deals with the heredity and variation of organisms) and the processes in which bacteria acquire resistance to antibiotics through genetic mutation (change in hereditary material). Her research with deoxyribonucleic acid (DNA) paved the way for greater understanding of bacteria and more effective treatment of disease. In 1964 Alexander was named president of the American Pediatric Society, making her one of the first women to head a national medical association.

Hattie Alexander developed a successful treatment for influenzal meningitis, a deadly childhood disease.

The work of microbiologist and pediatrician Hattie Alexander helped doctors to conquer influenzal meningitis, a childhood disease that at one time was nearly always fatal. By experimenting with the bacterium that causes the disease, Alexander was able to develop a serum that could be used as a cure. Incorporating her serum with the use of certain drugs, she designed a complete line of treatment against the illness. Alexander's strategy, which was soon adopted by doctors, resulted in a tremendous decrease in deaths from influenzal meningitis.

Average student shines in research

Alexander was born on April 5, 1901, in Baltimore, Maryland, the second of eight children. Her parents were Elsie May (Townsend) Alexander and William Bain Alexander, a merchant. She attended public schools and then enrolled in Goucher College in Baltimore on a partial scholarship. At Goucher she excelled in sports, but she was only an average student in her course work. Alexander graduated from Goucher with a bachelor of arts degree in 1923.

For the next three years Alexander worked as a bacteriologist (a scientist who studies bacteria, microorganisms that carry disease). She held positions at the U.S. Public Health Service laboratory in Washington, D.C., and at a branch laboratory of the Maryland Public Health Service. Alexander's impressive research skills convinced the faculty at Johns Hopkins University in Baltimore to admit her to the school's medical program. She earned a medical degree in 1930.

Observes fatal disease

While serving an internship (training program) at the Harriet Lane Home of Johns Hopkins Hospital, Alexander became interested in influenzal meningitis, a usually fatal childhood disease. Influenzal meningitis was caused by *Hemophilus influenzae,* a bacterium that produces inflammation of the meninges (the membranes surrounding the brain and spinal cord). In 1931 Alexander began a second internship at the Babies Hospital of the Columbia-Presbyterian Medical Center in New York City. During this time she witnessed firsthand the inability of doctors to save babies who had contracted influenzal meningitis.

Advances in career

After Alexander completed her medical training in 1933, she held a variety of positions at the Babies Hospital, the Vanderbilt Clinic of the Columbia-Presbyterian Medical Center, and the Columbia University College of Physicians and Surgeons. She was promoted to attending pediatrician at the Babies Hospital and the Vanderbilt Clinic in 1951. Alexander rose steadily through the teaching ranks, becoming an associate professor in 1948 and a full professor in 1958. She retired as professor emerita (an honorary title) in 1966.

Develops anti-influenzal serum

Alexander's early research focused on deriving a serum that would be effective against influenzal meningitis. Serums from animals that have been exposed to a specific disease-producing bacterium often contain antibodies and can be used for immunizing humans. Alexander knew that attempts to develop an anti-influenzal serum from horses had been unsuccessful. Researchers at the Rockefeller Institute in New York City, however, had been able to prepare a rabbit serum for the treatment of pneumonia, another bacterial disease. Alexander then experimented with rabbit serums. By 1939 she was able to announce the development of a serum for curing influenzal meningitis in infants.

Develops treatment for disease

During the early 1940s Alexander experimented with the use of drugs in combination with rabbit serum in the treatment of influenzal meningitis. Within the next two years, deaths

Makes Progress in Antibiotics

Microbiologist and pediatrician Hattie Alexander conducted research in drug treatment for influenzal meningitis that led to advances in the use of antibiotics. After working with influenza bacteria in the laboratory, Alexander realized that antibiotics do not provide a permanent defense against bacteria. She was among the first researchers to recognize that bacteria are able to develop a resistance to antibiotics through genetic mutation. Later she became a pioneer in research on deoxyribonucleic acid (DNA), the substance in the nucleus of a gene that bears the genetic "blueprint" of an organism. By 1950, with the help of laboratory work conducted by Grace Leidy, Alexander was able to alter the genetic code of *Hemophilus influenzae* by manipulating its DNA. She went on to extend this line of research to other bacteria and to viruses.

from the disease dropped by 80 percent. With improvements in accurately diagnosing (identifying through the observation of symptoms) the disease and developing a standard treatment, the number of deaths from influenzal meningitis continued to fall over the next several years. In recognition of her research on influenzal meningitis, Alexander received the E. Mead Johnson Award for research in pediatrics from the American Academy of Pediatrics (1942) and the Elizabeth Blackwell Award from the New York Infirmary (1956). In 1961 she became the first woman to win the Oscar B. Hunter Memorial Award of the American Therapeutic Society.

Active in professional groups

In addition to her hospital service and research and teaching career, Alexander was a member of the influenza commission for the office the U.S. Secretary of War (1941–1945). She was also a consultant to the New York City Department of Health (1958–1960), and served on the medical board of the Presbyterian Hospital of the Columbia-Presbyterian Medical Center (1959). After chairing the governing council of the American Pediatric Society (1956–1957) and serving as vice president (1959–1960), she became president of the society in 1964.

Alexander was a member of several other pediatric associations, as well as the Society for Experimental Biology and Medicine, the American Association for the Advancement of Science, the New York Academy of Medicine, and many professional and scientific bodies. During her career she published nearly one hundred fifty papers and numerous chapters in textbooks on microbiology and pediatrics.

Further Reading
New York Times (obituary), June 25, 1968, p. 41.

Notable American Women: The Modern Period, Belknap, 1980, pp. 10–11.

Rustin, McIntosh, "Hattie Alexander," *Pediatrics,* Volume 42, 1968, p. 554.

Aristotle

*Born 384 B.C.
Stagira, Greece
Died 322 B.C.
Chalcis, Greece*

Aristotle is regarded as one of the great philosophers of the ancient world. He is known for providing the basis for many modern scientific fields. Aristotle was particularly active in the study of biology (a branch of knowledge that deals with living organisms). He devised a classification system for plants and animals that was used for more than two thousand years. During the course of his work Aristotle separated and defined the major areas of study of his time—physics (a science that deals with the interactions of energy and matter), metaphysics (a branch of philosophy concerned with the nature of reality), rhetoric (the art of speaking or writing effectively), poetics (poetic theory and practice), and logic (the science of reasoning).

One of the greatest thinkers in history, Greek philosopher and scientist Aristotle laid the foundation for centuries of Western thought.

Studies at Plato's academy

Aristotle was born in 384 B.C., in Stagira, a small town in northern Greece. (Stagira is located on the three-pronged peninsula known as the Chalcidice and borders the northern coast of

The ancient Greek philosopher Aristotle established some of the basic tools of investigation and classification used by scientists today. Aristotle's work included collecting and dissecting plants and animals and observing the behavior of organisms. Using this information, he founded a system of classification for the approximately one thousand species then known. In fact, Aristotle's system was used by scientists until Swedish naturalist Carl Linnaeus developed a more comprehensive method in the eighteenth century. A few of Aristotle's ideas, however, may have hindered science. For instance, until the 1600s scientists and the Roman Catholic Church accepted his belief that the Earth was the center of the universe. This theory contributed to the persecution of scientists such as Galileo Galilei, who attempted to correct Aristotle's error.

the Aegean Sea.) Farther north lay the ancient city of Macedonia, a small kingdom that rose during Aristotle's lifetime to rule the entire Mediterranean world and beyond. Aristotle's father, Nicomachus, was the royal doctor for the Macedonian king, Amyntas III (d. 336 B.C.). Young Aristotle is believed to have spent part of his childhood living with his father at the royal court in the Macedonian capital of Pella. As a doctor's son, he was probably trained in first aid techniques and basic drug therapy from an early age. This training may have contributed to his love of science in general and to his special interest in biology.

When Aristotle was only ten years old, his father died. The boy was then brought up by an older relative named Proxenus. At age seventeen Aristotle was sent to the most famous school in Greece, the Academy at Athens, which was headed by the Greek philosopher Plato (c. 427 B.C.–347 B.C.). Plato's teachings were concerned with theories of morality and existence, as well as the nature of good and evil. Aristotle spent twenty years at the Academy, winning recognition as Plato's most brilliant student. Gradually, however, Aristotle shifted his interest from Platonic ideas to more concrete studies. Determined to learn how the world actually worked, he studied the unique nature of human beings, plants, animals, and other physical objects. Unlike Plato, Aristotle focused on the nature and function of living things rather than philosophic explanations for their existence.

Begins observing nature

In 359 B.C., Philip II (382–336 B.C.) succeeded his father Amyntas III to become king of Macedonia. A powerful leader,

Philip quickly initiated a period of Macedonian expansion. He improved the army, captured nearby Greek cities, and attempted to increase Greek influence on Macedonian culture. Philip's growing power heightened tensions between Athens and Macedonia, and Aristotle's family connections to the Macedonian court may have proved problematic. For instance, when Plato died in 347 B.C., Aristotle probably expected to replace him as head of the Academy. This honor went to someone else, however, perhaps because of anti-Macedonian feelings in Athens.

After Plato's death Aristotle left Athens and settled near the Greek city Atarneus in northern Asia Minor (now Turkey). The city's ruler, Hermias, was an avid student of philosophy who had supported the Academy. He invited Aristotle and other

Aristotle lectures Alexander the Great. King Philip of Macedonia asked Aristotle to tutor his son, who later became one of the most famous monarchs in the ancient world. Reproduced by permission of Archive Photos, Inc.

scholars to set up a similar school in nearby Assos. Aristotle then began the work that truly reflected his own interests. He observed animals in their natural environments and carefully recorded his findings in a large collection of notes and longer writings now called the *Historia Animalium* ("Researches into Animals"). The work describes in great detail the bodies, habitats, and behavior of an astonishing variety of animals.

Tutors Alexander the Great

After Hermias was overthrown in 344 B.C., Aristotle moved to the nearby island of Lesbos, located in the Aegean Sea. At Lesbos he continued animal studies with the help of a young student named Theophrastus (c. 372 B.C.–c. 287 B.C.) While continuing his biological studies, Aristotle also worked on other writings, including *Politics*, his famous treatise about different systems of government. Soon after Aristotle moved to Lesbos, however, Philip asked him to return to Macedonia to oversee the education of his son Alexander. By now the leading intellectual in Greece, Aristotle thus began instructing the boy who would become Alexander the Great (356 B.C.–323 B.C.). Aristotle tutored Alexander for about three years.

Little is known about the relationship between the scientist and the future conqueror, but Aristotle's influence on Alexander does not seem to have been strong. In *Politics*, Aristotle argues that monarchy (absolute rule by a single person) is not an ideal form of government. He also expresses his disapproval of imperialism (a policy of expanding and winning new territory). Yet his young student, the son of a monarch, grew up to be a strong monarch himself. Alexander went on to become one of history's great imperialists, not only conquering most of the known world, but also spreading Greek culture in the process.

Founds Lyceum

Around 339 B.C., Aristotle left Macedonia and returned to live at his family home in Stagira. He was accompanied by

Theophrastus and other scholars for whom he had been a tutor. Four years later, in 335 B.C., Aristotle returned to Athens and opened his own school, which rivaled Plato's Academy. Since it was located at the temple of Apollo the Lycian (Lycia was an area in Asia Minor associated with the god Apollo), the school was called the Lyceum. Because Aristotle often walked around a covered courtyard, or *peripatos,* while lecturing, he and his followers were called "Peripatetics." Aristotle also used his family wealth to start an important library and natural science museum at the Lyceum. The library later served as a model for others, which were established after Aristotle's death.

As head of the Lyceum, Aristotle expanded his research into the various branches of science, literature, philosophy, and history. Unlike Plato, who focused solely on abstract theories, Aristotle's main goal at the Lyceum was collecting and classifying information. Because of Aristotle's emphasis on research, some modern scholars have called the Lyceum the first true university.

Linnaeus Invents Taxonomy

Due to his work collecting and classifying living things, Greek philosopher Aristotle has often been credited with establishing the basic tools of modern science. During his lifetime Aristotle devised a classification system for plants and animals that was used for more than 2,000 years. This method of organization is now called taxonomy. The system devised by Aristotle was eventually reinvented by Swedish naturalist Carl Linnaeus (1707–1778). Linnaeus gave every plant and animal two Latin names, one for the species and the other for the group, or genus, within the species. Although Linnaeus started with only two kingdoms, contemporary classifiers have expanded this number to five kingdoms. The science of taxonomy has changed since the time of Aristotle, and it continues to expand with the evolution of modern science.

Creates classification system

One of Aristotle's most influential achievements in the field of biology was to create a classification system for all known plants and animals. He organized various groups on the basis of their physical characteristics, such as animals with backbones and those with no backbones. Aristotle's system was used for more than 2,000 years. During the 1700s increased knowledge of the living things of other lands revealed that Aristotle's theories were too limited. Swedish scientist Carl Linnaeus (see entry in volume four) eventually invented a more detailed system, known as taxonomy, which became the basis for the method of classification used by modern scientists.

In 323 B.C., when Alexander the Great died, anti-Macedonian feelings again swept through Athens. Aristotle left Athens, as he put it, "to save the Athenians from sinning a second time against philosophy." The first "sin" had been the execution, in 399 B.C., of the philosopher Socrates, who had been Plato's teacher and mentor. Aristotle retreated to his family's property on the island of Euboea, located in Chalcis, Greece.

Influences modern science

Until the end of the Middle Ages (around A.D 1500), the volume of Aristotle's writings, combined with the force of his ideas—even when wrong—made him the most trusted and respected voice on virtually every scientific topic. Some of his theories, such as his belief that the Earth was the center of the universe, were far from accurate. But his pioneering work in biology guided many great scientists, including nineteenth-century British naturalist Charles Darwin (1809–1882), and his achievements continue to influence modern scientific theory. During his lifetime, Aristotle married Hermias's niece, Pythias, and the couple had two children. Aristotle died in 322 B.C. at Euboea.

Further Reading

Aristotle, *The Basic Writings of Aristotle,* edited by Richard McKeon, Random House, 1941.

Barnes, Jonathan, *Aristotle,* Oxford University Press, 1982.

Ferguson, John, *Aristotle,* Twayne, 1972.

Satyendranath Bose

Born January 1, 1894
Calcutta, India
Died February 4, 1974
Calcutta, India

Satyendranath Bose was an Indian physicist who gained attention in the 1920s when he developed a new statistical method to explain the black body radiation law of German physicist Max Planck (see entry in volume three). The black body law is part of quantum theory, which states that radiant energy is transmitted in the form of discrete units (quanta). Bose's new method was important because it provided the basis for a theory formulated by German-born American physicist Albert Einstein (see entry in volume one). According to Einstein, light energy not only consists of individual quanta (particles later known as photons), but also demonstrates wavelike properties. In honor of Bose's contribution to the field, the boson was named after him. (The boson is a category of the subatomic particle studied in quantum physics using the Bose-Einstein statistical approach.)

Satyendranath Bose confirmed Albert Einstein's ideas about the behavior of photons.

Indian physicist Satyendranath Bose developed a new statistical method. He unified ideas about the structure of light energy that had been formulated by physicists Max Planck and Albert Einstein. Bose's work confirmed Einstein's idea that photons behave according to rules similar to those governing atoms and are able to gain and lose electrons. Einstein, in turn, used Bose's ideas as the basis for Bose-Einstein statistics. This mathematical approach is used to predict the location and energy values of certain subatomic particles. One such particle discovered with this method was named the *boson* in honor of Bose.

Studies under leading physicist

Born in Calcutta, India, on January 1, 1894, Bose was the son of Surendranath Bose and Amodini Raichaudhuri. His father was an accountant who later founded the East India Chemical and Pharmaceutical Works. Bose's education began in English-language schools set up by the British during their colonial reign over India (1857–1947). During the resurgence of Bengali nationalism in 1907, Bose's father transferred his son to a Bengali language school. (Bengal is a region in the northeast section of the Indian peninsula.) After graduating from secondary school, Bose attended Presidency College in Calcutta, where he studied under noted Indian physicist Jagadischandra Bose (1858–1937; no relation to Satyendranath). In 1915 Bose continued his postgraduate studies at the university, finishing first in his class with a master of science degree in mathematics. Two years later he became a lecturer in the physics department in the science college at the University of Calcutta. Established in 1914, the college was the first in India to offer advanced science studies.

Bose's natural gifts in mathematics soon became apparent when he coauthored, with Meghnad Saha, two papers on the equation of state. (The equation of state is the mathematical relationship between the pressure, density, and temperature of a substance.) In 1919 Bose and Saha coedited one of the first anthologies in English of Einstein's scientific papers on the theory of relativity. (The theory of relativity states the relationship between measurements taken from two systems in motion relative to each other.) The following year Bose published his first paper on quantum statistics in *Philosophical Magazine*.

The Evolution of Physical Theory

Until the late nineteenth century, the field of physics was divided between energy and matter. Most scientists agreed that matter is composed of tiny individual particles with measurable mass. They considered the atom to be the ultimate particle that comprises all matter. On the other hand, they determined that energy does not consist of matter, but instead is a force that can cause a change of position in matter. Most forms of energy were thought to travel through space as waves.

By the turn of the century, however, this theory was being questioned by such scientists as the German-born American physicist Albert Einstein. In an analysis of the photoelectric effect, Einstein showed that the emission of electrons from a metal that has been exposed to light can best be explained by assuming that light consists of tiny "packages" of energy. The "size" of each package is determined by the wavelength of the light.

Lays foundation for quantum statistics

In 1921 Bose accepted a position as a professor at the University of Dacca, a newly established institution in East Bengal. At Dacca Bose focused on the statistics of photons (a quantum of electromagnetic energy). In the first decade of the twentieth century, two new ideas were presented to explain the behavior of light energy. One was the black body radiation law, which Planck proposed in 1900. A black body is an object that absorbs all frequencies, or levels, of light when it is heated and gives off all frequencies as it cools. Planck's law explained this behavior by stating that the energy of a black body is carried away in individual, measurable packages called quanta.

In 1905 Einstein used Planck's concept to explain the photoelectric effect (the release of electrons from a metal when a light is shined on it). Since the discovery of this effect in 1888, scientists had been puzzled by the fact that the number of electrons released was determined not by the intensity of light but by its color (wavelength). Einstein suggested that the photon has an atomic structure made up of a measurable (quantum) amount of electromagnetic energy. The energy of a quantum of light is determined by its wavelength. When the energy reaches a certain level, it is absorbed by electrons in the metal, giving them the power to be released from the metal object or surface.

Receives support from Einstein

Bose contemplated Planck's law for a long time before he devised a new theory for quantum mathematics. To show that Einstein's model and Planck's law were both correct, Bose used an approach that treated radiation as an ideal gas. (An ideal gas is a substance that maintains a constant relationship between its pressure, volume, and density.) By 1923 he had submitted a paper on his theory to *Philosophical Magazine,* but the piece was rejected. Bose was persistent, however, and sent the article to Einstein along with a letter requesting his assistance. Einstein was impressed with Bose's ideas. Essentially, Bose had succeeded in proving Einstein's proposal, whereas Einstein himself and others had failed. With Einstein's endorsement and translation into German, Bose's paper, called "Planck's Law and the Hypothesis of Light Quanta," was published in *Zeitschrift Für Physik* in 1924.

Bose had concentrated primarily on the mathematical aspects of his work. Therefore he did not foresee its far-reaching effects on the field of physics, especially the area of electrodynamics (the study of the interaction of electrical currents with magnets or other currents). As a result, Bose failed to gain the international recognition that came to such famous physicists as Planck and Einstein. These two researchers built on Bose's work to develop the foundation for Bose-Einstein statistics. It was the first of two approaches to quantum physics that determined the distribution of certain subatomic particles among the various possible energy values. Depending on the approach used, the particles that adhere to these mathematical laws are known as bosons (named after Bose) or fermions. Fermions were named for Italian physicist Enrico Fermi (see entry in volume one), the developer of the second approach.

Receives awards and honors

Although Einstein's support led Bose to leave India for two years to study in Germany and France, he never fulfilled his dream of working with Einstein. In fact, the two scientists had only one brief personal meeting. In 1926 Bose returned to Dacca and became a professor of physics. Because he was dedicated to teaching, he produced only twenty-six original papers. His work focused on mathematical statistics, electromagnetic properties of the ionosphere, X-ray crystallography, thermoluminescence, and the unified field theory.

Bose was appointed as the Khaira Professor of Physics at Calcutta University in 1945. In 1956 he became vice chancellor of Visva-Bharati University, which was established by Nobel Prize-winning poet Rabindranath Tagore (1861–1941). Bose was elected to the Royal Society in 1958 and was appointed a national professor by the Indian government in 1959. He also founded the Science Association of Bengali, which helped popularize science in India. Bose served in the Indian parliament (1952–1958) and was president of the National Institute of Sciences of India. Bose was also among a group of pioneering nationalist scientists and intellectuals who helped lead the Indian independence movement against British colonial rule. In 1914 Bose married Ushabala Ghosh, with whom he had two sons and five daughters. Bose died on February 4, 1974, in Calcutta.

Further Reading

Blanpied, William A., "Satyendranath Bose: Co-Founder of Quantum Statistics," *American Journal of Physics,* Volume 40, 1972, pp. 1212–20.

Dictionary of Scientific Biography, Scribner's, 1978, p. 325.

Sharma, Jagadish, "Satyendranath Bose," *Physics Today,* April 1974, pp. 129–31.

Tycho Brahe

Born December 14, 1546
Knudstrup, Scania, Denmark
(now in Sweden)
Died October 24, 1601
Bohemia (now a region
in Czechoslovakia)

Tycho Brahe
recorded celestial
observations that
greatly advanced
the knowledge of
the universe.

Portrait: Reproduced
by permission of the
Library of Congress.

Tycho (sometimes referred to as "Tyge") Brahe was a colorful figure in sixteenth-century astronomy (the study of objects outside the earth's atmosphere) who established a standard of careful scientific observation of the universe. Supported by a number of royal patrons (wealthy people who provide funds for scientific or creative projects), he built an elaborate astronomical observatory containing a number of tools for making accurate observations of the planets and stars. At this observatory, Brahe and his followers catalogued an enormous amount of astronomical data, all without the use of a telescope (an instrument for viewing distant objects), which was not invented until 1609. The information gathered by Brahe influenced a number of developments, most importantly the formulation of the laws of planetary motion (the movement of the planets) by Johannes Kepler (see entry in volume four).

Abandons career chosen by family

Brahe was born on December 14, 1546, into an ancient noble family in Knudstrup, Scania, Denmark (a city that is now in Sweden). He was the eldest son among the ten children of Otto and Beate Bille Brahe. When Brahe was born his father was an adviser to Christian III (1503–1539), the king of Denmark. When Tycho was only a year old, he was adopted (some sources say he was actually kidnaped) by his father's childless brother, Jorgen Brahe. The young boy then lived with his prosperous uncle on a country estate at Tostrup.

Beginning at the age seven, Brahe was tutored in Latin, basic math, reading, and writing. When he turned thirteen, he was sent to the University of Copenhagen to study philosophy and rhetoric (the art of speaking and writing effectively). Brahe was supposed to follow family tradition and become a statesman, but it was soon apparent that he would make his own career decisions. On August 21, 1560, the young man witnessed a solar eclipse (a phenomenon that occurs when the view of the Sun is blocked by the Moon). He was so fascinated by the event that he began to study mathematics and astronomy. In 1562 Brahe went to the University of Leipzig in Germany, a major center for the study of astronomy. To please his family, he studied law during the day, but at night he pursued his interest in astronomy.

Begins astronomical observations

In August 1563, Brahe made his first recorded observation, on the unusually close positions of the planets Jupiter and Saturn. To his annoyance, this event occurred a month before

IMPACT

Tycho Brahe was an influential sixteenth-century Danish astronomer. He is best known for making extremely accurate observations of the stars and planets without the use of a telescope. When Brahe observed the movement of a comet in 1577 he also disproved the ancient idea of physical structures holding up the planets. Furthermore, his diligent observation of the celestial bodies improved the accuracy of the calendar and predictions of astronomical events such as an eclipse. The astronomer made his greatest impact, however, through his assistant Johannes Kepler, who used Brahe's observations of the planets to develop the laws of planetary motion.

Without a Telescope

The telescope was invented in 1609—eight years after the death of Tycho Brahe—by famous Italian astronomer Galileo Galilei (see entry in volume four). Called the refractor telescope, the instrument caused a revolution in the field of astronomy. The telescope had an object glass that bent light rays to a focus near the eye, where a second lens, or eyepiece, then magnified the image. The telescope enabled astronomers to observe celestial bodies that could not easily be seen with the naked eye. Using the telescope, Galileo made many important astronomical discoveries, including the fact that the Milky Way was made up of individual stars. (The Milky Way is the galaxy of which the Sun and Moon are part and which appears as a luminous band of light in the night sky.) In contrast to Galileo, Brahe had to use simple measuring devices and previously published astronomy books for his observations. Because these resources were often inaccurate, Brahe relied mostly on his own diligence—and his own eyes. Historians speculate that Brahe would have made astonishing discoveries with the aid of a telescope.

it was supposed to happen. After pondering the situation, the young astronomer discovered major flaws in all of the tables then available on the topic of celestial movement. Brahe therefore concluded that only through continuous and systematic observation of heavenly bodies could celestial motion be accurately predicted. At the time this was a bold idea.

Brahe then set out to obtain astronomical instruments that would allow him to make more accurate measurements and predictions. Eight years after Brahe's death the Italian astronomer Galileo Galilei (see entry in volume four) developed the first popular telescope for making astronomical observations. Yet Brahe had to conduct his work with simple tools, such as measuring devices that relied on the naked eye. As he gained experience in astronomy, he became convinced that no device, no matter how well made, could guarantee error-free measurement. Consequently, the young astronomer designed mathematic tables to adjust his measurements for these built-in errors.

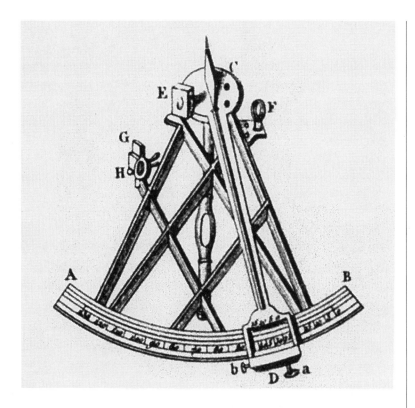

Observes star in 1572

In 1570 Brahe returned to Denmark to visit his ailing father, who later died. Having inherited some family property, Brahe moved into Heridsvad Abbey, where he set up a makeshift observatory. Now free from family intervention in his career choice, he could openly study astronomy. Brahe's first major observation came in 1572, when he discovered an extremely bright new star, now known to have been a super-nova (exploding star) in the constellation (group of stars) of Cassiopeia. With a sextant (an instrument used for observing altitudes of celestial bodies) and several other measuring instruments he had constructed, Brahe recorded the movement and color change of the star and roughly calculated its distance. For eighteen months he systematically recorded his observations of the star until it disappeared from view in March 1574.

Scholars urged Brahe to publish his findings, but noble-men rarely spent their time writing books in those days. When other astronomers began publishing incorrect data on the bright star he first observed in 1572, however, Brahe felt it was necessary to issue his own account. Brahe's book, *De Nova Stella* ("On the New Star"), published in 1573, thrust him into the forefront of astronomy. Brahe's observations were far superior to any others known at the time. Brahe caused a revolution in thinking on the location of planets and stars by estimating that the star was located at a distance much farther than the Moon. His work on the new star was so detailed that many people began to refer to the object as "Tycho's star."

Disproves "planetary spheres" theory

For three years, at the request of King Frederick II of Denmark (1534–1588), Brahe lectured at the University of Copenhagen on planetary motion. The king then made Brahe ruler of the small island of Ven and its inhabitants. As the landlord of an entire village and about forty farms, he could collect taxes. Brahe used the money to construct a castle, which he called 'Uraniborg' after Urania, the muse of astronomy. (The muses were nine sisters in Greek mythology who presided over song and poetry and the arts and sciences.) He also built and equipped an observatory called Sjarneborg, which was completed in 1580. Sjarneborg became the first true astronomical observatory in history. It attracted scholars and scientists from throughout Europe who came to visit and work with the respected astronomer.

For the next twenty years, Brahe and his students charted the course of the planets and catalogued more than a thousand stars without the aid of a telescope. Brahe's observations were extremely accurate, allowing him to estimate the length of the year to within a second. His scientific findings would later influence the calendar reform instituted by Pope Gregory XIII (1502–1585) in 1582. Among Brahe's most important observations during this time was the sighting of the comet of 1577. Brahe was one of the first people to view a comet as a natural event, rather than a religious or magical sign of doom.

Brahe's observations brought him to conclusions that contradicted traditional scientific thought. Since the time of the ancient Greek philosopher Aristotle (see entry), for instance, many scientists had believed that the Earth was the center of the universe. According to this theory, the Sun, planets, and other stars revolved around the Earth. It was also commonly thought that the planets circled the Earth on physical structures called "planetary spheres." Brahe's measurements showed that the path of the 1577 comet was not circular, but elongated. This meant that it would have to pass through the "spheres" that carried the planets, which was virtually impossible.

In 1543 the Polish astronomer Nicholas Copernicus (see entry in volume four) had presented a new view of the universe in which the Sun was circled by the planets. This idea was consistent with Brahe's findings, but for various reasons—including religious beliefs— Brahe would not support the Copernican system. He tried to reconcile his beliefs with his observations by proposing a solar system in which all the planets orbited the Sun. At the same time, according to Brahe, the Sun orbited the Earth and the celestial sphere (a structure he thought contained all the stars) made a single rotation each day.

Presents Tychonic system

Brahe presented his theory of planetary movement, popularly known as the "Tychonic System," in a 1583 work entitled *Astronomic Instauratae Progymnasmata* ("The New Astronomy"). Although his theory was never widely accepted, Brahe changed the practice of astronomy with his claim that heavenly bodies must be systematically observed over time in order to extend knowledge. From this point onward, new theories were not accepted by the scientific community unless they could be supported by observations. Because of Brahe, astronomy became a practical science as opposed to being based on theory.

Takes Kepler as an assistant

After Frederick II died in 1588, Brahe fell out of favor with the new king and left Denmark for Bohemia (now a

A Colorful Figure

Tycho Brahe is remembered as a highly colorful figure who, according to many accounts, was arrogant and egotistical about his scientific knowledge. This attitude may have contributed to a significant event that took place when he was only nineteen—an event that had little to do with astronomy. On December 10, 1566, Brahe and mathematician Marderup Parsberg got into an argument at a party, perhaps over a mathematical point. On December 27 they quarreled again and decided to settle their argument with a duel (one-to-one combat with swords) two days later. Brahe suffered the greatest injury, losing part of his nose to a swipe of Parsberg's sword. From then on, he wore a gold and silver shield over his nose to conceal the injury. It is said that Brahe constructed this "false nose" himself and always carried a small container of wax to reaffix it when it came unhinged.

In addition to his unusual appearance, Brahe's personal life was unconventional. He fell in love with a working-class woman named Christine, whom he never married. Nevertheless, the couple lived happily together for many years and had eight children. Brahe was also interested in alchemy (a medieval chemical science that sought to turn common metals into gold) and astrology (the belief that the position of stars affects human events).

region in Czechoslovakia). Once he had settled in Bohemia and set up another observatory, Brahe made contact with Kepler. The course of scientific history was changed forever because of the two men's meeting. Kepler had just written an influential book on the distances of the planets from the Sun (based on the Copernican system) and he sent a copy to Brahe. Though Brahe and Kepler differed in their views of the organization of the universe, they shared a mutual admiration. Kepler also realized that Brahe was aging and that no one had yet tapped the vast knowledge and information he had accumulated during decades of observation. Kepler approached Brahe about their working together, and Brahe eagerly accepted him as an assistant in 1600.

For the next year Kepler sorted through Brahe's volumes of observations and worked with him on his *Progymnasmata* and *Rudolphine Tables* (charts of calculations on planetary movements and distances). By this time, Brahe was already very weak. Within a few months he was near death. He willed his life's work to Kepler, imploring his assistant to finish the *Tables* on his own. Because of this union with Kepler, Brahe's work lived on after his death. His painstaking observations enabled Kepler to formulate the laws of planetary motion. These laws became the foundation of modern astronomy, which is based on regular and systematic celestial observation.

Further Reading

Dreyer, J. L. E., *Tycho Brahe: A Picture of Scientific Life and Work in the Sixteenth Century,* Adam & Charles Black, 1890; revised, 1963.

Lodge, Oliver, *Pioneers of Science,* St. Martin's Press, 1913.

Ronan, Colin, *The Astronomers,* Hill & Wang, 1964.

Williams, Henry Smith, *The Great Astronomers,* Newton Publishing Co., 1932.

Paul Ching-Wu Chu

Born December 2, 1941
Hunan Province, China

Paul Ching-Wu Chu has led the race to develop a high-temperature superconductor.

P aul Ching-Wu Chu is one of the best-known superconductivity scientists in the world. In 1987 Chu and a team of physicists discovered materials capable of conducting electricity at temperatures significantly higher than had previously been recorded. Scientists had been competing for decades to find a practical superconductor (a material that conducts electricity with no loss of energy) that performs at or near room temperature. Most superconductors work at extremely cold temperatures, making them too expensive to produce for commercial use. *New York Times* science writer James Gleick once predicted that practical-use superconductors would initiate "a turning point in scientific history ... a new age of electricity—a world of absurdly cheap power and trains floating in the grips of magnets." After making his initial discovery, Chu became caught up in an international competition among scientists to produce superconductors at even warmer temperatures.

Educated in Taiwan and United States

Chu was born in the Hunan Province of China on December 2, 1941, and grew up in the island nation of Taiwan. Graduating from Cheng Kung University with a bachelor of science degree in 1962, he moved to the United States to attend Fordham University in the Bronx, New York. After earning a master of science degree at Fordham, Chu went on to the University of California at San Diego in 1965. When he completed a doctorate in physics in 1968 he worked as a research assistant under superconducting expert Bernd T. Matthias (1918–1980). That same year Chu married May P. Chern, with whom he has two children, Claire and Albert. In 1970 Chu took a position as assistant professor of physics at Cleveland State University in Ohio. He became professor of physics at the University of Houston, Texas, in 1979. Nine years later Chu was named director of the Texas Center for Superconductivity.

Joins superconductor race

In 1986, while reading a scientific journal, Chu discovered a report from Nobel prize-winning researchers K. Alex Müller (1927–) and Johannes Georg Bednorz (1950–). The two scientists described the construction of a complex ceramic material at the IBM research laboratory in Zurich, Switzerland. The new material was proven to work as a superconductor in temperatures up to 35 Kelvin. (A temperature of 0 Kelvin, or K, is equivalent to minus 460 degrees Fahrenheit or minus 273 degrees Celsius.) The article inspired Chu and his colleagues to break that new barrier and make scientific history.

Superconductivity

Superconductivity occurs in many metals and organic materials when they are cooled to temperatures close to 0 Kelvin, or K (known as absolute zero). In 1911 Dutch scientist Heike Kammerlingh Onnes (1853–1926) observed superconductivity with mercury. The mercury had been cooled to near absolute zero with the use of liquid helium, a light gaseous element that is rare and quite costly. Since then, scientists had searched for cheaper materials that could perform the same feats of magnetism and conductivity at higher temperatures. Their goal was to find a material that would act as a superconductor at temperatures above 77 K. Then they could use liquid nitrogen (the liquid form of nitrogen gas), which boils at 77 K and can be carried in a Styrofoam cup, as a coolant in place of expensive helium. Because nitrogen makes up 78 percent of air, it is abundant and inexpensive. Thus superconductivity would be transformed to a potentially cheap means of generating, transmitting, storing, and using electrical power.

Makes history

Chu decided to join the search for a new and cheaper method of superconductivity. He worked with a group of colleagues at the University of Houston and a team from the University of Alabama in Huntsville, which was headed by Chu's former graduate student, Mau-Kwen Wu. By 1987 the scientists had discovered that a mixture of metals and rare earth oxides was capable of superconducting electricity at temperatures as warm as 98 K. This measurement far surpassed temperatures reached by Müller and Bednorz only a year earlier. The key ingredients, yttrium, barium, and copper, were later patented by Chu as compound 1–2–3.

On March 18, 1987, the world's top physicists gathered in New York City for the annual meeting of the American Physical Society. Chu gave a report on compound 1–2–3, while other researchers revealed that rare earth-based oxide ceramics could superconduct at extremely high temperatures. Suddenly the meeting became front-page news. One journalist described the gathering as "the Woodstock of physics." Some experiments have since suggested that the behavior of oxide superconductors like compound 1–2–3 may pose problems. Nevertheless, there is no question that Chu's breakthrough was a turning point in the history of superconductivity. It was hailed as a major step toward creating room-temperature superconductivity, which has become a kind of "holy grail" of science. Some scientists predict that room-temperature superconductivity, once achieved, will be as revolutionary as the invention of the transistor or the light bulb. Many envision numerous uses for this new superconductor—among them

Mammoth Superconductor Project Fails

During the 1980s scientists envisioned using superconductors to build better particle accelerators. A massive superconducting super collider (also referred to as "SSC") project was started in Waxahachie, Texas. Housed in a 53-mile, race-track-shaped tunnel 150 feet underground, the SSC was designed to answer a question that has stymied scientists since ancient times: What is the fundamental nature of matter? As part of the project's original plan, the SSC had a very generous budget. Unfortunately, because prototype superconducting magnets did not work as well as expected, the cost of the project exceeded the original estimate of $4.5 billion. Ultimately the venture was budgeted at $11 billion, but after six years of construction problems and cost overruns it was only 20 percent completed. Amounting to little more than an impressive hole in the ground, the SSC had become a monumental failure. In 1993, after spending more than $2 billion, Congress appropriated $640 million to dismantle the project.

faster and cheaper transportation, improved computer technology, and less expensive medical diagnostic imaging machines.

The race continues

Chu's findings were published in *Physical Review Letters* on March 2, 1987, and immediately set off a chain reaction of experiments. Scientists around the world duplicated the results, many of them over a weekend. Despite his incredible success, however, Chu did not slow his search for even better superconductors. He created an entirely new level of competition in September 1993 when he announced that his labs had developed a superconducting material at 153 K. His new record did not stand for long. Only one week later a French-Russian team claimed to have created a superconductor at 157 K. Energized by such fast-paced competition, Chu bounced back the next month with the discovery of a 164 K superconductor. Looking forward to even better developments, Chu shared his enthusiasm for the search with J. Madeleine Nash of *Time* magazine: "It's really exciting. Everything is moving fast, really fast."

Honored for groundbreaking work

In addition to his teaching and research positions, Chu has held posts at the National Aeronautics and Space Administration (NASA) Marshall Space Flight Center in Huntsville, Alabama, and the Los Alamos Science Lab in Los Alamos, New Mexico. He is also a member of the American Physical Society, the American Academy of Arts and Sciences, and the National Academy of Science. Chu's groundbreaking research has earned him a number of honors and awards. He received a National Medal of Science Award from the National Academy of Science in 1988. He was also honored with a NASA achievement award in 1987, the International Prize for new materials from the American Physical Society in 1988, and the Superconductivity Excellence Award from the World Congress on Superconductivity in 1994. In 1990 *U.S. News and World Report* named Chu the best researcher in the United States.

Further Reading

Dahl, Per Fridtjof, *Superconductivity: Its Historical Roots and Development from Mercury to the Ceramic Oxides,* American Institute of Physics, 1992.

Mayo, Jonathan L., *Superconductivity: The Threshold of a New Technology,* Tab Books, Inc., 1988.

Newsweek, December 19, 1988, p. 63.

New York Times, August 16, 1987, p. 29.

Physics Today, April 1987, pp. 17–23.

Popular Science, July 1987, pp. 54–58, 97.

Science, March 27, 1987, p. 1571.

Science News, January 10, 1987, p. 23; August 15, 1987, pp. 106–9.

Time, May 11, 1987, pp. 64–75; October 18, 1993, p. 85.

Alice Eastwood

Born January 19, 1859
Toronto, Ontario, Canada

Died October 30, 1953
San Francisco, California

A lice Eastwood was a dedicated botanist (a biologist who studies plants) who had a impressive and challenging career. One of the top plant specialists of her time, she never hesitated in her search for specimens (samples), sometimes during trips that involved hardships. Even the disastrous San Francisco earthquake and fire of 1906 did not dampen Eastwood's enthusiasm. As caretaker of the California Academy of Science herbarium (a collection of dried plant specimens), Eastwood revived hundreds of irreplaceable specimens after the quake. Afterward she rebuilt the herbarium collection and the botanical library, adding more than 340,000 items during the four decades between 1912 and her death in 1953.

Pursues interest in plants

Eastwood was born in Toronto, Canada, on January 19, 1859. Her parents, Eliza Jane Gowdey and Colin Eastwood, emigrated to Canada from Northern Ireland. When Eastwood

Leading twentieth-century botanist Alice Eastwood collected and classified thousands of plants.

Alice Eastwood was a dedicated botanist who specialized in studying the flowering plants of the Colorado and California mountains. She is best known for her work in restoring the herbarium at the California Academy of Sciences after the San Francisco earthquake and fire of 1906. In spite of Eastwood's heroic efforts, only a small number of specimens survived the disaster. Vowing to rebuild the herbarium, she set about carefully collecting specimens on extensive expeditions in California and Canada. There is little doubt that without Eastwood's courage and hard work, the valuable plant collection at the Academy would not exist today. As a direct result of her efforts the institution eventually became an important research center.

was six years old, her mother died. The child was sent to live with her uncle, Dr. William Eastwood, on a country estate near Toronto. She was free to roam where she pleased, and in her wanderings she became interested in the surrounding flora (plant life). William Eastwood taught his niece all about the plants, including their Latin scientific names.

After being enrolled at the Oshawa Convent in Toronto, Eastwood moved to Denver, Colorado, with her father. Although she was able to attend public high school, family financial problems forced her to hold a job. For a time Eastwood worked as a nursemaid (a woman employed to look after children) at the home of a French family. She read books from her employers' large library, and increased her knowledge of plants when she accompanied them on trips to the mountains. The ambitious Eastwood also continued to excel in her studies. In spite of her added responsibilities, she graduated at the top of her class in 1879.

Although Eastwood dreamed of becoming a botanist, she knew that she needed to find a way to support herself. She took a teaching job at East Denver High School, where she worked for the next ten years. Eastwood's salary was small, but she still saved enough money during the school year to spend her summers in the Rocky Mountains of Colorado exploring for plants. Because of her thorough knowledge of Colorado flora, Eastwood became a local legend in Denver. Her extensive collections from those days later became the basis for the University of Colorado Herbarium in Boulder.

Becomes a full-time botanist

In 1890, when a successful real estate investment guaranteed Eastwood a small income, she was finally able to devote

all her time to botany. She made one of her first trips as a full-time botanist to San Francisco, California, to visit the California Academy of Sciences. At the Academy, Eastwood met T. S. and Katherine Brandegee, a husband-wife botanist team. Impressed with Eastwood's knowledge and enthusiasm, the Brandegees invited her to work at the Academy. Although Eastwood was reluctant to leave Colorado and the Rocky Mountains, she finally accepted the position in 1892.

Eastwood was immediately elected a member of the Academy and began assisting in the herbarium. When the Brandegees left San Francisco in 1894, Eastwood was named curator (caretaker) of the herbarium. She soon began organizing and enlarging the collection, spending her own money to buy new specimens and embarking on numerous collecting

The herbarium and flower conservatory at Golden Gate Park in San Francisco. Alice Eastwood used her own money to rebuild the herbarium after the 1906 earthquake and fire. Reproduced by permission of Stephen L. Saks. Photo Researchers, Inc.

Classification System

When botanist Alice Eastwood restored the herbarium at the California Academy of Sciences, she used a system designed by Carolus Linnaeus, the founder of modern botany. In 1753 Linnaeus composed a hierarchical classification of plants, creating a nomenclature that continues to be used today. According to Linnaeus's system, which is called taxonomy, every plant is given two scientific names in Latin, one for the species and the other for the group within the species. Today, taxonomy is an even more sophisticated and precise science in which plant kingdoms are divided into classes.

expeditions of her own. Eastwood made some of her most important trips to the Sierra and Coast mountain ranges of California, where she documented the plant life. In the Coast range, she even discovered a new species of daisy, which T. S. Brandegee named *Eastwoodia* in her honor.

Rescues and rebuilds herbarium

One of Eastwood's projects at the herbarium was to organize the most valuable plant specimens so that they could be easily rescued in an emergency. Her concern for the safety of this precious collection seemed to be a premonition of the disastrous earthquake that struck San Francisco on April 18, 1906. When Eastwood arrived at the Academy after the tremors, she found the building locked and partially destroyed. Her greatest concern at the moment was the devastating fire consuming the city that had been caused by the earthquake. Determined to rescue her best specimens from the approaching flames, Eastwood asked a friend to assist her in retrieving the plants. Luckily, the pair managed to save 1,211 specimens.

After the earthquake and fire, Eastwood used her own money to rebuild the herbarium. Working independently on the project for six years, she undertook several field trips to the Sierra and Coast mountains. She was especially careful to verify that plants were labeled accurately. She even traveled to institutions in England and France to compare her specimens to the original plants used for classification. Finally, in 1912, the Academy was rebuilt on a new site in Golden Gate Park in San Francisco and Eastwood was asked to found a new herbarium. During her lifetime it was renamed the Alice Eastwood Herbarium.

Continues dynamic career

Between 1912 and 1949, Eastwood increased the plant collection at the Academy by more than 340,000 specimens. Her duties, however, did not interrupt her expeditions. In 1914, at the age of fifty-five, Eastwood undertook an expedition to the Yukon territory in Alaska to collect samples. She continued these rugged trips, with the help of a guide, into the 1930s. Throughout her career, Eastwood wrote nearly three hundred articles and published a book titled *Popular Flora of Denver, Colorado* in 1893. In 1950 she was named the honorary president of the International Botanical Congress in Sweden. Remaining active until the end of her life, Eastwood died on October 30, 1953, at the age of ninety-four.

Further Reading

Bailey, Martha J., *American Women in Science: A Biographical Dictionary,* ABC-Clio, 1994, pp. 95–96.

Bonta, Marcia Myers, *Women in the Field: America's Pioneering Women Naturalists,* Texas A & M University Press, 1991, pp. 93–102.

Notable American Women: The Modern Period, Harvard University Press, 1980, pp. 216–17.

Ogilvie, Marilyn Bailey, *Women in Science: Antiquity through the Nineteenth Century,* MIT Press, 1986, pp. 79–80.

Charles Elton

Born March 29, 1900
Manchester, England
Died May 1, 1991

Biologist and zoologist Charles Elton helped to establish animal ecology as a distinct field of scientific study.

Charles Sutherland Elton was a respected biologist and zoologist who helped to establish the scientific field of animal ecology (the study of animals and their environment). Elton's entire career was dedicated to advancing the understanding of the effects of the environment on animal populations. He wrote a number of influential books on the subject, including *Animal Ecology,* published in 1927. In his works Elton outlined the now commonly used concepts of ecosystems, food chains, and renewable resources. One of his most significant contributions to science was the establishment of the Bureau of Animal Population. The internationally acclaimed research center was dedicated to the study of ecology and the interaction of animal populations.

Influenced by brother

Elton was born on March 29, 1900, in Manchester, England, to Oliver and Letitia Maynard MacColl Elton. Shortly after Elton's birth, his family moved to the east coast of England, where his father joined the staff of Liverpool University. In Liverpool young Elton began to develop a strong interest in nature, a curiosity encouraged by his older brother, Geoffrey Yorke Elton. Geoffrey fostered Charles's appreciation of the beauty of the world around him and taught him to carefully observe all living things. When Geoffrey died suddenly at age thirty-three, Elton was devastated. From that point onward, he dedicated his life to observing and understanding the natural world.

Participates in Arctic expeditions

In 1918 Elton entered New College at Oxford University, where he studied zoology (the science of animal life) under English zoologist Julian Sorell Huxley (1887–1975). Huxley was the grandson of English biologist Thomas Henry Huxley (1825–1895), a defender of the theory of evolution, which was formulated by Charles Darwin (see entry in volume one). In 1921, while Eastwood was still an undergraduate, he was invited to assist Huxley on the first Arctic expedition to Spitsbergen (a group of islands in the Arctic, north of Norway) sponsored by Oxford. Because of extreme weather conditions, however, the project was not a complete success. Two years later Elton was invited to participate in the second Spitsbergen expedition. This time he found only nine dry-land invertebrates (animals lacking a spinal column) out of a possible sixty or more known species for that location.

On a third expedition to Spitsbergen in 1924, Elton was placed in charge of all scientific work. He spent most of his time working from the base camp, conducting a general survey of animal life in the region. During this trip Elton nearly

IMPACT

Biologist and zoologist Charles Elton spent his career studying the factors that affect animal populations in particular ecosystems. His work led to a new field of science known as animal ecology. Elton's ideas, which he published in such books as *Animal Ecology* (1927) and *Pattern of Animal Communities* (1966), inspired many other scientists to study in the field of animal ecology. For instance, pioneering American conservationist Aldo Leopold based his influential study, *Game Management* (1933), on Elton's findings about animal populations. To stimulate more research in the field of animal ecology, Elton helped to found and operate the Bureau of Animal Population.

lost his life when he fell through the ice. It is thought that the event may have actually aided his scientific endeavors by increasing his awareness of the impact of accidental occurrences in the population dynamics of animal life. (Population dynamics is the rise or fall of the number of individuals in a specific area.)

After the 1924 expedition, Huxley suggested that Elton write a book on his findings in the Arctic. The young zoologist completed the work in less than three months. Published in 1927, *Animal Ecology* became a milestone in the fields of biology and ecology. Previously, the study of ecology had focused only on plant life. In his book Elton established methods and concepts that detailed the role of animals in the environment. His work led to the creation of the new field of animal ecology.

Studies animal populations

After graduating from Oxford University with high honors in 1922, Elton stayed on as a part-time zoology instructor. This position enabled him to continue researching and documenting animal population fluctuations, or changes. In 1929 Elton was hired as a full-time faculty member, and he held the post for sixteen years. Four years later he was appointed a biological consultant to the Hudson's Bay Company (an international retail and manufacturing firm). For the next five years Elton conducted studies on the population changes of fur-bearing animals and their prey (other animals taken as food). With the help of George Binney of the Hudson's Bay Company, Elton established a simple yet sophisticated recording system that provided reports from hundreds of observers from a wide geographic area. Combined with the company's archives (historical records), this data eventually enabled Elton to trace the population fluctuation of the Canadian lynx back to 1736.

Elton also continued to participate in academic expeditions, traveling to the Lapland region of northern Norway, Sweden, and Finland in 1930. In addition, he undertook studies closer to home, recording thousands of animal species in

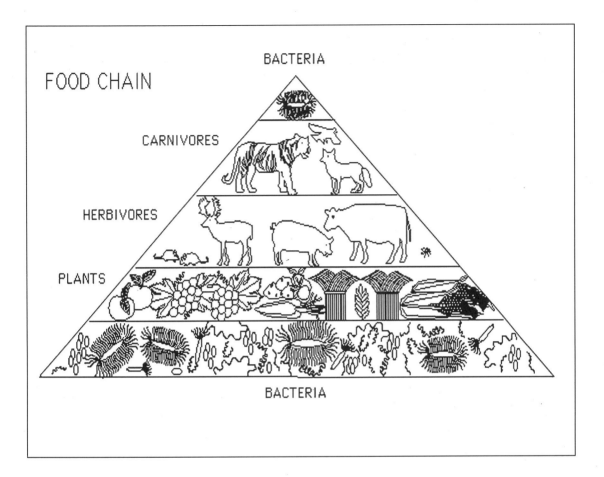

FOOD CHAIN

BACTERIA

CARNIVORES

HERBIVORES

PLANTS

BACTERIA

Wytham Woods near Oxford. This project became known as the Wytham Biological Survey. Throughout his career Elton published a number of influential books. His work during the Lapland expedition resulted in *Animal Ecology and Evolution* (1930) and *Moles, Mice and Lemmings* (1942). The results of his investigations at Wytham Woods were published in *Patterns of Animal Communities* (1966).

Introduces major theories

During his career Elton formulated important concepts that are now used in environmental studies. He was the first person to define ecosystems (the interdependent unit of a population and its natural environment) and to explain the differ-

The ecological pyramid. Charles Elton developed the idea of the ecological pyramid to demonstrate the number of organisms that are involved at each level of a resource system. Illustration reproduced by permission of Gale.

ence between renewable and nonrenewable resources in such a system. He also made important contributions to the theory of a "food chain"—the idea that all living things are dependent on other living things for their food. According to this concept, an increase or decrease of a particular population anywhere along the food chain affects all other populations.

Similarly, Elton developed the idea of the ecological pyramid to demonstrate the number of organisms that are involved at each level of a resource system. For example, in a food pyramid a large number of plants provide food for a smaller number of plant-eating animals. In turn, the plant-eating animals become food for a smaller number of meat-eating animals. Throughout his career, Elton stressed the importance of studying an entire community within a specific habitat (environment where animals and plants live and grow). According to Elton, this is the only way to understand the complex interactions taking place in nature.

Establishes Bureau of Animal Population

In addition to his other professional activities, Elton was instrumental in establishing the Bureau of Animal Population (BAP), which was created in 1932. The BAP was designed to provide scientists with a place to study population dynamics with a minimum of distraction. The bureau served as an important international research center for the next thirty-five years. During this time Elton was actively involved in raising funds. Although the institution operated on a small budget, the members conducted high-quality research because Elton maintained a strict focus on the goals of the BAP. Nearly three years after its establishment, the center became an official unit of Oxford University.

Supports war effort

In the late 1930s Britain was faced with the possibility of a war with Germany. The government notified all scientists that they would be excused from military service in order to carry out any research that was useful to the war effort. Rather than wait for the government to request the assistance of the BAP, Elton quickly devised a plan that would keep the institution in operation. He notified the Agricultural Research Council (ARC) that the BAP was ready to investigate the loss of food to rodents (small mammals such as mice and squirrels) on the battlefield and in military storage areas. Elton's plan was approved by the ARC in August 1939, and the university began the project shortly after the outbreak of World War II (1939–1945). Elton's team was highly successful in controlling the rodent problem in the military food supply, and much of the BAP research was published by the ARC after the war.

Under Elton's leadership, the BAP acquired a reputation as a first-rate center for study and research. Elton made many friends within the national and international ecological network, but he tended to stay out of the political arena at Oxford. Consequently, when the university began considering the possibility of closing the BAP, Elton had no political supporters. After Elton retired in 1967, university officials decided to make BAP scientists part of the Oxford zoology department. Scientists who had worked with the BAP and Elton were astounded that such a successful research center would cease to exist. After the institute was closed, Elton managed to keep the BAP library intact and to preserve a space to continue the Wytham Biological Survey.

The Food Chain

Charles Elton made important contributions to the concept of the food chain, the process through which food energy is transferred from plants through a series of organisms. The "links" in the chain usually involve at least four levels called trophics (groups of organisms). The first trophic is plants. Herbivores (animals that eat plants) form the second trophic level. The third level consists of primary carnivores (animal-eating animals like wolves) that eat herbivores, and at the fourth level are animals (like killer whales) that eat primary carnivores. Food chains overlap because many organisms consume more than one type of food, so that these chains can look more like food webs. By the mid-twentieth century animal ecologists became concerned about damage being done to food chains as a result of environmental pollution caused by humans.

Receives awards and honors

Elton was an important figure in scientific and environmental circles. He is credited with helping to found the Nature Conservancy in England in 1948. He was also an honorary member of the American Academy of Arts and Sciences. His influence on animal ecology studies was strengthened by his role as founder and editor of the professional publication *Journal of Animal Ecology.* Even though Elton was a modest man, he received a number of prestigious honors for his work. He was awarded the Gold Medal of the Linnaean Society in 1967. He also received the Darwin Medal of the Royal Society in 1970 and the Edward W. Browning Award for conservation in 1977. During his lifetime, Elton was married twice, and had two children from his second marriage.

Further Reading

Crowcroft, Peter, *Elton's Ecologists: A History of the Bureau of Animal Population,* University of Chicago Press, 1991.

Eblen, Ruth A., and William R. Eblen, eds. *The Encyclopedia of the Environment,* Houghton Mifflin, 1994, pp. 192–93.

Vernoff, Edward, *The International Dictionary of Twentieth Century Biography,* New American Library, 1987.

René Geronimo Favaloro

Born in 1923
La Plata, Argentina

Surgeon René Geronimo Favaloro was one of the pioneers of heart bypass surgery. Favaloro's technique uses a transplanted saphenous vein (one of two veins near the surface of the leg) to act as a bypass around a blocked or damaged section of a coronary artery (the vessel that carries blood from the heart through the body). Heart bypass surgery has become one of the most common and successful treatments for patients suffering from blocked arteries. Favaloro trained hundreds of doctors in the procedure. He also established the Institute of Cardiology and Cardiovascular Surgery in Buenos Aires, Argentina, one of the leading medical teaching facilities in Latin America. Favaloro is considered a hero by both his medical colleagues and the people of Argentina.

René Geronimo Favaloro developed the use of heart bypass surgery as a standard treatment for patients suffering from blocked coronary arteries.

Works as country doctor

Favaloro was born in La Plata, Argentina, to working-class parents named Juan and Ida. He attended the National

Heart surgeon René Geronimo Favaloro pioneered the use of heart bypass surgery as a common treatment for people suffering from blocked arteries. The procedure involves transplanting the saphenous vein from the patient's leg into the heart. The transplanted vein acts as a bypass around a blocked or damaged section of a coronary artery. Favaloro played a major role in spreading knowledge of bypass surgery when he trained hundreds of doctors in the use of the technique. He is also the founder of the Institute of Cardiology and Cardiovascular Surgery in his native country of Argentina.

College and Medical School at the University of La Plata, receiving a medical degree in 1949. He served an internship and residency (two training programs for doctors) at Instituto General San Martin in La Plata, where he was later appointed to his first staff position. The young doctor also attended an advanced course at Rawson Hospital in Buenos Aires, Argentina. In 1962, after twelve years of practicing medicine in the remote pampas (vast prairie regions) of Argentina, he visited the Cleveland Clinic in Ohio. Favaloro was curious about the latest surgical techniques being developed in the thoracic (chest cavity) and cardiovascular (heart and circulatory system) department at the renowned medical research center.

Myocardial revascularization introduced

At the time of Favaloro's visit, Cleveland Clinic researchers were experimenting with myocardial revascularization (increasing a restricted blood supply to the heart). The scientists were searching for a way to prevent health problems caused by hardening of the arteries, also known as arteriosclerosis. Arteriosclerosis results from the accumulation of cholesterol (a fatty substance) on the walls of blood vessels. Built-up cholesterol traps calcium (a metallic element present in certain compounds in the human body). In turn, calcium hardens the vessel walls and narrows the blood passageway. Narrowing, or blocking, of coronary arteries (atherosclerosis) prevents circulation of blood to the heart, causing coronary diseases.

Myocardial revascularization had been attempted before World War II (1939–1945), with little success. The primary reason was inadequate diagnosis (identifying a disease from its symptoms), which was based mainly on assumptions drawn from the symptoms of the patient. In 1957 Dr. F. Mason Sones Jr. of the Cleveland Clinic began searching for a simple diagnostic tool to accurately identify diseases of the coronary arteries. He eventually developed angiography, a test in which dye is inserted into the arteries, exposing on X rays the exact location of blockages.

The technique enabled doctors to both give more precise diagnostic evaluations and identify the individual needs of patients. In addition, doctors could arrive at a relatively accurate prognosis (prediction of recovery) and prescribe the appropriate therapy. The tool became the primary means of selecting candidates for bypass surgery.

Helps pioneer heart bypass surgery

When Favaloro joined the Cleveland Clinic as an observer, myocardial revascularization was still in the experimental stage. Two techniques were being used. One was the pericardial patch graft, in which the wall of a blocked artery is opened and "patched" with part of a leg vein in an attempt to increase the size of the artery. The other technique was the mammary artery implant. This involved inserting the mammary artery from the chest into the wall of the left ventricle (chamber) of the heart, thus supplying blood to be pumped into the blood vessels.

After Favaloro completed his observations he studied all the information he could find on revascularization. In his now-famous 1967 bypass operation, he removed the saphenous vein from the patient's leg and inserted one end of the vein into the aorta (large artery above the heart). He then inserted the other end into an artery below an obstructed area. As the result of this procedure, blood flow was fully restored.

Establishes bypass as standard

Although Favaloro was the first surgeon to perform a full bypass at the Cleveland Clinic, he was not the first to use the procedure. David Sabiston Jr., working at Duke University in

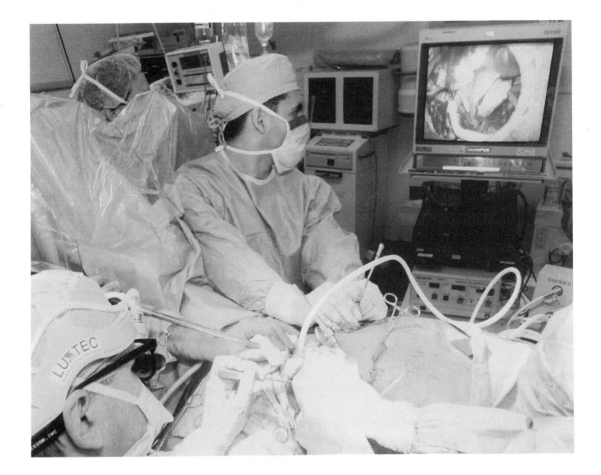

North Carolina, unsuccessfully performed the first known human bypass in 1962. The first successful bypass was achieved by H. Edward Garrett in 1964. Both operations were used in emergency situations. Neither Sabiston or Garrett developed the procedure as a standard treatment, nor did they publish any details about the procedure for almost ten years. Favaloro fully intended to adopt his first bypass operation as a standard procedure for appropriate candidates, however, and he documented his findings in a paper that was published in 1968.

Trains others in new procedure

By 1970 Favaloro and the Cleveland Clinic cardiovascular team had performed more than one thousand bypass opera-

Heart bypass surgery, which was perfected by surgeon René Geronimo Favaloro, is considered by doctors to be an effective method for curing the problem of blocked coronary arteries. Nevertheless, some critics claim that the procedure is overused, causing many patients to pay for unnecessary surgery. A less costly alternative to a heart bypass is angioplasty, which was first performed by Andreas Gruentzig on September 16, 1977. This technique involves inserting a tiny balloon into the restricted artery and inflating the balloon to compress the blockage material against the artery wall. Although angioplasty was considered safe, doctors became concerned about the high rate of restinosis (renarrowing of the vein) following the procedure. As a result, bypass surgery remained the choice of most surgeons because its results lasted longer. By the late 1990s, extensive research was being conducted on the use of laser energy after angioplasty to stimulate the growth of new blood vessels. This technique is called percutaneous transmyocardial laser revascularization.

tions, of which nearly a quarter were multiple bypasses. The death rate was an astonishingly low 4.2 percent. In 1971, at the height of his surgical career, Favaloro returned to Buenos Aires and established the Favaloro Foundation for the teaching of bypass surgery. In 1992, after twenty years of dedication and hard work, Favaloro's lifelong dream was fulfilled with the completion of the ten-story, $55 million Institute of Cardiology and Cardiovascular Surgery, one of the finest medical teaching institutes in Latin America. By then his programs had trained more than three hundred heart surgeons, half of whom were Latin American. Favaloro's team had also performed thousands of bypass operations.

Remains in forefront

Favaloro is a member of the Medical Society of La Plata and the Societe Internationale de Chirurgie. In 1967 he was elected a fellow of the American College of Surgeons, which made him an honorary fellow in 1990. Favaloro is considered a hero by both his medical colleagues and the people of his nation, who frequently suggest him as a presidential candidate. Despite this recognition, Favaloro still identifies himself as a simple country doctor. During the 1990s he continued to advocate the need for well-trained family physicians who place the welfare of patients above reliance on high technology. Favaloro also remains one of the foremost authorities on bypass surgery. In 1998 he was a featured speaker at the Thirteenth World Congress of Cardiology in Rio de Janeiro, Brazil.

Further Reading

Favaloro, René Geronimo, *The Challenging Dream of Heart Surgery: From the Pampas to Cleveland,* Little, Brown, 1994.

"Interview with Dr. René Favaloro," *OSDE Binario,* 1997. [Online] Available http://www.osde.com, August 12, 1998.

"Percutaneous Transmyocardial Laser Revascularization." [Online] Available http://home.att.net/jwilentz/laser.html, September 14, 1998.

"Saphenous Bridge Creator Speaks on the Advances of Cardiac Surgery," Rio de Janeiro, Brazil: XIII World Congress of Cardiology, April 26–30, 1998. [Online] Available http://babelfish.altavista.digital.com, August 12, 1998.

Benjamin Franklin

Born January 17, 1706
Boston, Massachusetts

Died April 17, 1790
Philadelphia, Pennsylvania

T hroughout his life, Benjamin Franklin wore many hats, including printer, writer, civic leader, inventor, politician, and ambassador. His experiments and writings on electricity, however, made him an internationally famous eighteenth-century American. Before Franklin's work, electricity was considered a bizarre force that was interesting mainly for use in entertainment. Franklin's numerous investigations and findings established the study of electricity as a valid scientific pursuit.

Becomes an apprentice

Franklin was born on January 17, 1706, in Boston, which was at that time located in the British colony of Massachusetts. His father was Josiah Franklin and his mother was Abiah Folger. Because his family was poor, young Franklin did not receive a proper education. For instance, he attended the Boston Grammar School for only one year because his parents could not afford the tuition. Later he spent a year at George

Remembered as one of the founding fathers of the United States, Benjamin Franklin was also the first American to achieve an international reputation as a scientist.

Benjamin Franklin was a man of many talents. Although he had no formal education as a scientist, Franklin made important discoveries about the nature of electricity. He also introduced many of the terms now used in connection with the phenomenon, such as charge, conductor, and plus and minus charges. In his most famous experiment, Franklin attached a metal key to a kite and proved how an electrical charge is generated during a thunderstorm. His writings and experiments on electricity helped to establish the subject as a valid scientific pursuit. Franklin's scientific fame also helped pave the way for his later political and diplomatic career.

Brownell's English School, where he failed arithmetic. Luckily, Franklin's parents encouraged reading, thinking, and discussion, and the young man grew up in a educational environment. He began working at the age of ten as an apprentice (a person who learns by practical experience) in his father's chandlery shop (a place where candles are made).

Since Franklin enjoyed reading, his parents eventually decided that he should enter the printing trade. Therefore, at the age of twelve, he became an apprentice for his brother James, who ran a Boston newspaper called *The New England Courant*. James's printing shop was a center of social activity, which provided Ben with a constant flow of new ideas. Customers would often linger to discuss politics or religion, and they also brought books for him to borrow. During this time the ambitious young man improved his writing and editing talents. At the age of seventeen Franklin left Boston to seek his fortune elsewhere.

Settles in Philadelphia

Franklin finally settled in Philadelphia, Pennsylvania, in 1726. Three years later he purchased a failing newspaper, *The Pennsylvania Gazette,* which eventually reached a high circulation. In 1733 he also began publishing *Poor Richard's Almanack,* a collection of witty sayings and pieces of advice that he wrote under the pseudonym (pen name) of Richard Saunders. The *Almanack* was an instant and enduring success, selling more than ten thousand copies annually. The book contained Franklin's own formula for success. Sayings such as "Haste makes waste" and "God helps them that help themselves" provided a body of practical philosophy for English colonists to live by.

During the 1730s Franklin branched out into other projects. In 1736 he founded the Union Fire Company in Philadelphia. The industrious young man also started a police force and promoted the paving and lighting of city streets. Reflective of his lifelong love of reading, Franklin founded what was probably the first circulating library in America. Established in 1731, it was originally a subscription library to which members contributed an annual fee in return for the full use of books and pamphlets. In 1736 Franklin was appointed clerk (official in charge of records) of the Pennsylvania Assembly, where he gained valuable political experience over the next fifteen years.

Begins experimenting with electricity

During the 1740s scientists around the world were investigating static (accumulated) electricity. Franklin first witnessed this new force in a demonstration of the Leyden jar (a device used for producing electrical energy) in 1743. The Leyden jar was simply a bottle filled with water that had a stopper in an opening on one end. Through the stopper was inserted a metal rod that extended into the water. A machine was used to create a static electric charge that was stored in the jar. Anyone who touched the end of the charged rod received an electrical jolt. Public demonstrations, in which many people joined hands and received a shock at the same time, were highly popular at the time.

Franklin was so inspired by the Leyden jar that he tried his own experiments, thus beginning his career as an amateur scientist. Investigating the source of the electrical shock, he poured the charged water out of the jar into another bottle and discovered that the water no longer held a charge. Franklin suspected this result indicated that the glass itself had produced the shock. To verify his theory, Franklin took a window pane and placed a sheet of lead on each side. He electrified the lead, removed each sheet, and then tested the lead for a charge. Neither sheet gave a single spark, but the window pane had been charged. Franklin had unknowingly invented the electrical condenser, which later received its name from Italian

Invents Practical Devices

Benjamin Franklin was a great inventor who could turn ideas into practical, working items. One of his first major inventions was the Pennsylvania fireplace—now known as the Franklin stove—which was developed around 1740. Improving on an existing design, Franklin equipped the stove with a flue (a heat channel) that heats the air around it. The stove was highly efficient; Franklin claimed it made a room twice as warm as other stoves, even though it used only 25 percent of the usual amount of wood. Another popular Franklin invention was the bifocal eyeglass lens, in which the lower part of the lens is designed for near vision and the upper part for distant vision. Franklin is also credited with creating the rocking chair.

physicist Alessandro Volta (see entry in volume five). The condenser is now used in radios, televisions, telephones, radar systems, and many other devices.

Through further experiments, Franklin discovered that electricity is an independent force, which he called "electrical fire." According to Franklin, a substance with a shortage of electrical fire has a negative, or minus, electrical charge. An element with extra electrical charge has a positive, or plus, electrical charge. He believed that electricity flows from plus to minus, but scientists now know that the opposite is true. Franklin also introduced the important concept known as conservation of charge. (Conservation of charge states that for every amount of charge gained by one body, an equal amount of charge must be lost by another body.) The idea that the overall electrical energy in a system does not increase or decrease is now a fundamental law in science. Franklin introduced many other terms that still pertain to electricity, including battery, conductor, charge, and discharge. He also discovered that electricity moves particularly well through metals and water.

Performs kite experiment

Drawing a parallel between the sparking and crackling of the charged Leyden jar and the lightning and thunder that occur during a storm, Franklin wondered if there was an electrical charge in the sky. To test his idea he devised the Philadelphia experiment, which he published in a book that was widely read in Europe. According to the experiment plan, Franklin would erect a long metal rod atop Christ Church in Philadelphia. During a lightning storm the rod would conduct electricity to a sentry box (a guard station). A man standing on an insulated (protected) platform would then collect the electric charge.

After Franklin published his idea, however, another man used the plan to conduct his own experiment. On May 10, 1752, a French scientist named D'Alibard performed Franklin's test by charging a Leyden jar with lightning. Franklin later recognized D'Alibard as being the electricity pioneer. Franklin did receive credit for inventing the lightning rod (a metallic rod with one end embedded in the ground, which diverts electricity to the earth and protects buildings against fire caused by lightning). By 1782 there were four hundred lightning rods in Philadelphia.

While waiting for the lightning rod to be installed on Christ Church, Franklin came up with an idea for a faster way to get a conductor into the sky. He made a kite by tying a large silk handkerchief to two crossed wooden sticks. He attached a long silk thread to the kite that had a metal key tied at the end. Then he waited for a thunderstorm. During the storm the rain soaked the thread, making it an excellent conductor (an item that permits flow of electric current) that transmitted a static charge from the sky down to the key. When Franklin touched his knuckle to the key, a spark jumped from the key to his hand, thus proving the existence of electricity in the sky. Franklin also stored the electric charge in a Leyden jar.

Fortunately, Franklin had been wise enough to connect a ground wire to his key. (A ground wire diverts an electrical charge into the earth.) Two other scientists attempted to duplicate the experiment, but neglected to use a ground wire. The men were struck by lightning and killed.

Investigates other areas of science

Although Franklin was best known for his work in electricity, he investigated other areas as well. His interest in the weather led him to notice that weather patterns usually travel from west to east. He suggested that this was due to the circulation of air masses (large accumulations), thus establishing

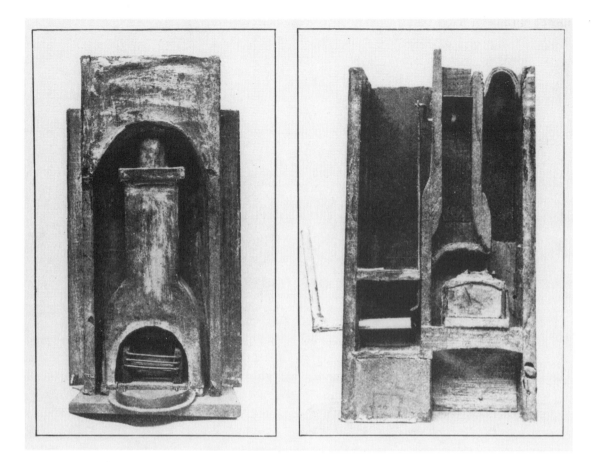

the meteorological concepts of high and low pressure in the atmosphere. Another of Franklin's interests was the sea. During his diplomatic career, Franklin journeyed across the Atlantic Ocean eight times. On these trips he made notes while observing the ocean waters. With the help of a sea captain, he created the first chart of the Gulf Stream (a warm current in the Atlantic Ocean). Franklin also devised a method of using a thermometer to gauge water temperature to determine if a ship was on course in the Gulf Stream.

Franklin introduced several innovations in the field of medicine. He was a strong supporter of regular exercise, particularly swimming. He believed in the importance of fresh air for good health, even though at the time many people thought night air and drafts caused disease. Expanding on his electrical studies, Franklin used electric shocks to treat people with paralysis (the loss of body movement); he eventually determined, however, that this treatment did not offer any permanent benefits. When smallpox inoculations were first introduced, Franklin warned against the practice. (Smallpox is a highly contagious, often fatal disease. Inoculation is the introduction of the disease-causing agent into the body in order to create an immunity.) After his own son died of the disease, however, he reversed his opinion and published a pamphlet on the importance of inoculation.

Enters international politics

In 1748 Franklin retired from business and science to devote the rest of his life to politics and diplomacy. Three years later he was elected to the Pennsylvania Assembly. In 1757 Franklin began his diplomatic duties when he was sent to England as a lobbyist (a person who represents a particular group in attempting to influence public officials). While in England, he tried to convince the British that the Stamp Act of 1765 was not a good way to obtain money from the American colonies. (The Stamp Act required that all newspapers, pamphlets, and other documents published in the colonies bear a stamp. Revenues from stamped items would be used for military defense.) Finally, in 1775, Franklin returned to America and joined the Second Continental Congress (the governing body of the Thirteen Colonies). He helped to draft the Declaration of Independence (a document that stated the American colonists' reasons for demanding freedom from Great Britain), which was completed in 1776.

After the start of the Revolutionary War (1775–1783; a rebellion by the American colonies against British rule), Franklin was sent to arrange an alliance with France against England. In 1778 he signed treaties with France that may have helped America win the Revolutionary War. Franklin also served on the peace commission that negotiated the 1783 Treaty of Paris, which ended the war. After he returned from France in 1785, Franklin was elected president of the Pennsylvania Executive Council.

Receives awards and honors

Franklin's experiments with electricity brought him great fame in America and Europe. Not only was he respected by the scientific community, he was also popular with the general public. Franklin spread his ideas through a number of writings, including articles in the leading scientific journal of the time, *Philosophical Transactions of the Royal Society.* In 1751 Franklin's papers on electricity were gathered and published in a ninety-page book in London. The Royal Society, a British scientific organization, awarded Franklin the Copley Medal in 1753 for his accomplishments and made him a member of the society in 1756. Franklin also received a number of honorary degrees from institutions such as Harvard University (1753), Yale University (1753), and Oxford University (1762).

During his lifetime, Franklin had an ongoing relationship with Deborah Reed, whom he never married because she had not been officially divorced from her husband. Franklin already had one son named William, born to an unknown mother, who joined the family. Franklin and Reed had two children of their own, a son named Francis (who died of smallpox) and a daughter named Sarah. During the last few years of his life, Franklin lived with Sarah and numerous grandchildren in a large house on Market Street in Philadelphia. He spent his last years completing his *Autobiography* (first published in 1868), which became a classic work in American literature. Franklin died in Philadelphia on April 17, 1790, at the age of eighty-five. His funeral was attended by approximately twenty thousand people, who came to mourn the passing of a great man.

Further Reading

Asimov, Isaac, *Asimov's Biographical Encyclopedia of Science and Technology,* 2nd rev. ed., Doubleday, 1982, pp. 177–79.

Dictionary of Scientific Biography, Volume 5, Scribner's, 1972, pp. 129–39.

Fleming, Thomas, *The Man Who Dared Lightning: A New Look at Benjamin Franklin,* William Morrow, 1970.

Franklin, Benjamin, *Benjamin Franklin's Autobiography,* edited by J. A. Leo Lemay and P. M. Zall, Norton, 1986.

Magill, Frank N., editor, *The Great Scientists,* Volume 5, Grolier, 1989, pp. 1–8.

Benjamin Franklin

Solomon Fuller

Born August 11, 1872
Monrovia, Liberia
Died January 16, 1953

Solomon Fuller was a pioneering African American psychiatrist during the first half of the twentieth century.

Solomon Fuller, the first African American psychiatrist, played a significant role in the development of modern psychiatry (a branch of medicine that deals with mental disorders). He was one of the first doctors in the United States to study both the physical and psychological (mental) symptoms of his patients. His work led to a better understanding of disorders such as Alzheimer's disease (an abnormal degeneration, or breaking down, of brain cells) and schizophrenia (a brain disorder that causes radical changes in behavior). During his career Fuller taught at the Boston University School of Medicine in Massachusetts and cofounded the neuropsychiatric unit of the Veterans Hospital at the Tuskegee Institute in Alabama. In recognition of Fuller's pioneering work as a psychiatrist, two mental health facilities were named in his honor.

Begins school in Africa

Fuller was born on August 11, 1872, in Monrovia, Liberia (a country in western Africa). His grandfather, John

62

Lewis Fuller, was a slave in America who bought his freedom and moved to Liberia. Solomon's father, also named Solomon, was a coffee planter and a government official in Liberia. His mother, Anna Ursala James, whose parents were physicians and missionaries, set up a school to teach her son and other area children.

At age ten Fuller entered the College Preparatory School of Monrovia, where he studied for the next six years. When he was seventeen he left Liberia to attend Livingstone College in North Carolina. Fuller graduated in 1893 and began studying medicine at Long Island College Hospital in New York. He then transferred to the Boston University School of Medicine, where he received a medical degree in 1897. Upon graduation, Fuller began an internship (training program) at the Westborough State Hospital in Massachusetts. After two years he became a pathologist (a researcher of diseases). Meanwhile, Fuller was also a faculty member at the Boston University School of Medicine, where he taught for the next thirty-four years.

Collects data on psychiatric disorders

Fuller's decision to pursue a career in neurology and psychiatry was influenced by a lecture given by neurologist S. Weir Mitchell at a meeting of the American Medico-Psychological Association prior to 1900. (A neurologist is a physician who deals with the nervous system.) Criticizing hospitals for not studying mental illness, Mitchell called for institutions to focus on both the pathological (diseases of the body) and the psychological disorders of their patients. Following Mitchell's advice, Fuller began collecting and analyzing data on patients with various mental disorders. To further his knowledge of psychiatric illnesses, Fuller began taking advanced courses at the Carnegie

IMPACT

Solomon Fuller was the first African American psychiatrist. He was also one of the first doctors in the United States to study both the physical and psychological symptoms of his patients. Fuller's work led to important advances in the understanding of disorders such as Alzheimer's disease and schizophrenia. Fuller is considered a pioneer because he focused on the physical causes of illnesses that affect the functioning of the mind. A respected psychiatrist, Fuller helped make the United States a leading center of psychiatric research and practice. Serving more than thirty years on the faculty of the Boston University School of Medicine, he also cofounded the neuropsychiatric unit of the Veterans Hospital at the Tuskegee Institute in Alabama.

Laboratory in New York in 1900. Four years later he went to Europe and studied under Emil Kraepelin (1856–1926) and Alois Alzheimer (1864–1915), two professors at the University of Munich in Germany.

After returning to the United States, Fuller continued his work at Westborough and Boston University, investigating a number of ailments affecting mental health. Fuller became known for his work on Alzheimer's disease. He also focused his research on the organic (based in the body) causes of disorders such as schizophrenia and manic-depressive psychosis (now called bipolar disorder; the disease causes opposite extremes in behavior). Fuller continued to practice psychiatry after his retirement from research and teaching.

Remembered as a pioneer

During his career Fuller helped develop the neuropsychiatric unit at the Veterans Administration Hospital in Tuskegee, Alabama, personally training the doctors who became heads of the department. His knowledge of the symptoms of syphilis (a contagious disease of the genital organs) later helped these doctors identify the disease in black veterans of World War II (1939–1945) who had been incorrectly diagnosed with psychiatric disorders.

In 1909 Fuller married Meta Vaux Warrick, a sculptor who studied under the famous French sculptor Auguste Rodin (1840–1917). Fuller and his wife had three sons. Though he became blind later in life, Fuller continued to work, treating patients and reading via talking books (audio recordings of printed texts). Respected during his lifetime by the medical community, Fuller is today remembered as a pioneer. The mental health facility at Boston University is now officially known as

the Dr. Solomon Carter Fuller Mental Health Center. In 1972 the American Psychiatric Association and the Black Psychiatrists of America established the Solomon Carter Fuller Institute.

An aerial view of the Tuskegee Institute in Alabama. Solomon Fuller cofounded the neuropsychiatric unit of the Veterans Hospital at the Institute. Reproduced by permission of Corbis-Bettmann.

Further Reading

Cobb, Montague W., "Solomon Carter Fuller, 1872–1953," *Journal of the National Medical Association,* September 1954, pp. 370–72.

McNamara, Owen J., "Solomon Carter Fuller," *Centerscope,* winter 1976, pp. 26–30.

Shapley, Robert H., "Solomon Carter Fuller," in *Psychoanalysis, Psychotherapy, and the New England Medical Scene, 1844–1944,* edited by George E. Gifford, Jr., Science History Publications/USA, 1978, pp. 181–95.

Robert C. Gallo

Born March 23, 1937
Waterbury, Connecticut

Robert C. Gallo has made important discoveries about AIDS, including the finding that the disease is caused by HIV.

Portrait: Reproduced by permission of Archive Photos, Inc.

American medical researcher Robert C. Gallo is considered the codiscoverer—along with French researcher Luc Montagnier at the Pasteur Institute in France—of the human immunodeficiency virus (HIV). Gallo established that the virus causes acquired immunodeficiency syndrome (AIDS), a breakthrough that Montagnier had not been able to make in his research. Gallo also developed a blood test for HIV that remains a central tool in efforts to control the disease. Before conducting AIDS research, Gallo discovered the human T-cell leukemia virus (HTLV). (A T cell is responsible for dealing with most viruses, as well as some bacteria and fungi in the human body; T cells are also involved in cancer detection.) He also recognized the human T-cell growth factor, which he called interleukin-2. Both of these findings laid the groundwork for the AIDS virus search.

Becomes medical researcher

Gallo was born in Waterbury, Connecticut, on March 23, 1937, to Francis Anton and Louise Mary (Ciancuilli) Gallo. As a young man, Gallo was deeply affected by the death of his sister, Judy, from childhood leukemia (a form of cancer caused by the increase of white cells in the blood). By the time he was ready to attend college, Gallo knew he wanted to become a biomedical researcher (a person who develops medicines based on the study of biology). In 1959 he graduated from Providence College in Rhode Island with a bachelor of science degree in biology. Gallo then attended Jefferson Medical College in Philadelphia, Pennsylvania, where he began his career in medical research. While he was still a medical student Gallo studied oxygen deprivation (a lack of oxygen) in coal miners, which led to his first scientific publication in 1962.

In 1961 Gallo married Mary Jane Hayes, a woman from his hometown whom he began dating in college. The couple later had two children. Gallo graduated from medical school in 1963. He then went to the University of Chicago in Illinois, a major center for the study of blood-cell biology, which had become the focus of his research. From 1963 to 1965 Gallo conducted experiments on the biosynthesis (creation of a compound by the body) of hemoglobin (the protein that carries oxygen in the blood).

Studies human retroviruses

In 1965 Gallo became a clinical associate at the National Institutes of Health (NIH) in Bethesda, Maryland. He spent most of his first year at the NIH caring for cancer patients. Dur-

IMPACT

American medical researcher Robert C. Gallo is one of the best-known scientists involved in the search for clues to the nature of acquired immunodeficiency syndrome (AIDS). His laboratory team at the National Cancer Institute was one of two research groups that initially identified the human immunodeficiency virus (HIV), the agent that causes AIDS. Gallo's team also developed a blood test for HIV that has become a valuable tool in the fight against the deadly disease. For many years Gallo was under investigation for allegations that his team stole information from a French AIDS research group. The charges were eventually dismissed, and Gallo has since continued to search for an AIDS cure.

ing that time Gallo observed some early successes at treating cancer patients with chemotherapy (the use of chemicals to control disease). In fact, children were being cured of the exact form of leukemia that had killed his sister almost twenty years earlier. In 1966 Gallo became a full-time researcher at NIH. He studied the enzymes (proteins that bring about biological reactions) involved in the creation of the components of deoxyribonucleic acid (DNA), the carrier of genetic information.

Expansion of the NIH and passage of the National Cancer Act in 1971 led to the creation of the Laboratory of Tumor Cell Biology at the National Cancer Institute (NCI), a division of the NIH. As head of the new laboratory, Gallo became intrigued with the possibility that certain kinds of cancer are caused by viruses (microorganisms or molecules that cause infections). He set up his new laboratory to study human retroviruses. (Retroviruses are viruses that possess the ability to penetrate other cells and splice their own genetic material into the genes of their hosts, eventually taking over all of the cells' reproductive functions.) At the time Gallo began his work, retroviruses had been found only in animals. Determined to discover whether retroviruses also exist in humans, he attempted to isolate a virus from victims of certain kinds of leukemia.

In 1975 Gallo and fellow researcher Robert E. Gallagher announced that they had identified a human leukemia virus. The scientists' victory was short-lived, however, because other laboratories were unable to replicate (reproduce) their findings. (When scientists achieve successful results in experiments, they send samples to other researchers for independent confirmation.) Independent researchers discovered that samples from the Gallo-Gallagher experiment had been contaminated by viruses from a monkey or a chimpanzee. As a result, the idea that a virus could cause cancer in humans was widely ridiculed in the scientific community.

Despite public humiliation and damage to his reputation, Gallo continued his efforts to isolate a human retrovirus. He turned his attention to T cells, the white blood cells that are an important part of the body's immune system. He finally developed a substance called T-cell growth factor (later called inter-leukin-2), which would preserve the cells outside the human body. T-cell growth factor was important because it enabled Gallo and his team to preserve cancerous T cells long enough to determine whether they contained a retrovirus. These techniques also allowed the researchers to isolate a previously unknown virus from a leukemia patient. Gallo named the human T-cell leukemia virus, or HTLV, and in 1981 he published his finding in the journal *Science*. This time his results were confirmed.

Develops AIDS blood test

In 1981 AIDS was identified by doctors in the United States. Because Gallo was experienced with viral research, he became an important figure in the effort to identify the cause of the deadly AIDS disease. Continuing his studies of HTLV, Gallo established that the T-cell growth factor could be transmitted by breast-feeding, sexual intercourse, and blood transfusions (the infusion of blood into the body). Finding that HTLV had these and other characteristics in common with facts then known about AIDS, Gallo became one of the first scientists to hypothesize that the disease was caused by a virus. He also observed that cancers caused by this virus were concentrated in Africa and the Caribbean. In 1982 the NCI formed an AIDS task force with Gallo as its head. In this capacity he made available to the scientific community the research methods he had developed for HTLV. Among the researchers whom Gallo provided with early technical assistance was Luc Montagnier at the Pasteur Institute in Paris, France.

Throughout 1983 Gallo tried to grow the AIDS virus in culture (samples produced in the laboratory). Although he used the same growth factor that had worked in creating HTLV, he had no success. Finally, Mikulas Popovic, a member of the Gallo team, developed a method to grow the virus in a line of T cells. The method basically consisted of mixing samples from various patients into a kind of a "cocktail." As many as ten different strains of the virus were used at a time, so there was a higher chance that patients could survive. This

Deadly Human Diseases

Throughout history, the human population has been struck by deadly disease strains. One of the most lethal recorded diseases was the pneumonic plague, or "Black Death" of 1347–1351, which produced a mortality rate of 100 percent. Victims of the Black Death could be identified by dark blotches on their skin. An extremely virulent modern disease, acquired immunodeficiency syndrome, or AIDS, was first reported in 1981 by researcher Robert C. Gallo. AIDS is caused by the human immunodeficiency virus, or HIV. In the early 1990s the World Health Organization (WHO) reported 345,553 HIV-positive infections worldwide and estimated that eight to ten million people were infected with HIV. There has not yet been a documented case of full recovery from AIDS.

innovation allowed Gallo to isolate a new virus. Observing similarities to the retroviruses he had previously found, Gallo called his discovery HTLV-3. In 1984 he and his colleagues published their findings in *Science*. The researchers established that HTLV-3 causes AIDS, and announced that they had developed a blood test for the virus.

Allegations overshadow accomplishments

Even though Gallo achieved an important feat in discovering the HTLV-3 virus, he was immersed in controversy for the next decade. Because there had been such a rush to find the cause for AIDS, both American and French teams had been working on the project. Almost a year before Gallo and his team made their discovery in 1984, Montagnier had identified a virus he called LAV. He was not able to prove, however, that it caused AIDS. Controversy erupted when the United States government denied the French team a patent for its AIDS test and awarded a patent to Gallo instead. The Pasteur Institute immediately challenged this decision in court.

The first stage of the dispute ended when Gallo and Montagnier agreed out of court to share credit for discovery of AIDS. An international committee renamed the virus HIV, and the American and French groups published an agreement about their contributions in a 1987 edition of the journal *Nature.* In 1990 the controversy opened up again, however, when a U.S. congressional committee forced the NIH to undertake an investigation of Gallo and his laboratory. The NIH found Gallo guilty only of misjudgment, but charged his partner Popovic with scientific misconduct. In 1992 the NIH investigation was taken over by the Office of Research Integrity (ORI) at the Department of Health and Human Services. The ORI found both Gallo and Popovic guilty of scientific misconduct. This decision renewed the legal threat from the Pasteur Institute, whose lawyers moved to claim all the accumulated royalties (percentage of profits) from the AIDS blood test. At that time royalties totaled approximately twenty million dollars.

Lawyers representing Gallo and Popovic brought their cases before an appeals board at the Department of Health and Human Services. Popovic's case was heard first, and in December 1993 the board announced that he had been cleared of all charges. Then the ORI withdrew all charges against Gallo for lack of proof. The ORI determined that prior to 1984 Gallo had successfully isolated other strains of the virus that were not similar to LAV. Many scientists now believe that Gallo's problems occurred as a result of the intense pressure on researchers to achieve results during the early years of the AIDS epidemic. They speculate that the LAV sample from the Pasteur Institute had somehow contaminated the mixture of AIDS viruses Popovic was using to find one strain that would survive in culture. Consequently, this strain was strong enough to survive and be identified by Gallo and Popovic for a second time.

Regains reputation

In 1995 Gallo made a triumphant return to the top of his field. Along with AIDS vaccine developer Robert Redfield and epidemiologist William Blattner, Gallo offered to form an AIDS research "dream team" for a sponsor willing to provide them with a research center. (An epidemiologist is a person who studies diseases across populations and areas.) After negotiations with representatives from Maryland, Pennsylvania, South Carolina, and Virginia, the scientists reached an agreement with the state of Maryland. Under the contract Gallo became director of the Institute of Human Virology (IHV) at the University of Maryland. He also remained head of the NCI laboratory.

In 1995 Gallo achieved another success. His lab at NCI discovered certain natural chemicals that are used by cells to block the AIDS virus from replicating in the human body. This was viewed as a major breakthrough because when drugs are used to fight AIDS, the virus eventually develops a resistance to the medicine. Using natural chemicals in the body could lead to much better results in stopping the virus. At the time Gallo declared that there might be a cure for AIDS within the next decade.

Gallo came one step closer to his goal in 1996, with the announcement that his team had successfully treated Kaposi's sarcoma (a type of skin cancer frequently occurring in AIDS patients). He treated the cancer with human chorionic gonadotropin (hCG), a hormone occurring in the female body during pregnancy. Gallo and his team found that the hormone actually caused cancer cells to destroy themselves. These findings led Gallo to study the effects of hCG on AIDS itself. After a period of public scandal and doubt, Gallo is once again regarded as the scientist who may be able to find a cure for AIDS. During the late 1990s the Gallo team and the IHV continued to conduct research and sponsor forums on finding a cure for AIDS and other diseases.

Receives awards and honors

In 1990 Gallo published *Virus Hunting,* a book in which he made many of the claims that were later supported by the appeals board during the AIDS controversy. Gallo was twice honored with the coveted Albert Lasker Award, in 1982 and 1986. He also received the American Cancer Society Medal of Honor in 1983, the Lucy Wortham Prize from the Society for Surgical Oncology in 1984, the Armand Hammer Cancer

Research Award in 1985, and the Gairdner Foundation International Award for Biomedical Research in 1987. Gallo has also received eleven honorary degrees.

Further Reading

"AIDS' Achilles' Heel?" *Newsweek,* November 4, 1996, p. 68.

Angier, Natalie, review of *Virus Hunting, New York Times Book Review,* March 24, 1991, p. 3.

Carey, John, "Bob Gallo's New Weapon against AIDS," *Business Week,* January 15, 1996, pp. 87–88.

Clines, Francis X., "New Start for Besieged Scientist," *New York Times,* March 11, 1997, pp. B7, B9.

Cohen, Jon, "HHS: Gallo Guilty of Misconduct," *Science,* January 1993, pp. 168–70.

Gallo, Robert C., "My Life Stalking AIDS," *Discover,* October 1989, pp. 31–34.

Gallo, Robert C., *Virus Hunting: AIDS, Cancer and the Human Retrovirus,* HarperCollins, 1991.

Gladwell, Malcolm, "At NIH, an Unprecedented Ethics Investigation," *Washington Post,* August 17, 1990, p. A8.

Gorman, Christine, "Victory at Last for a Beseiged Virus Hunter," *Time,* November 22, 1993, p. 61.

Institute of Human Virology. [Online] Available http://www.ihv.org, September 1, 1998.

Marshall, Eliot, "Gallo's Institute at the Last Hurdle," *Science,* March 8, 1996, p. 1359.

Radetsky, Peter, "Immune to a Plague," *Discover,* June 1997, p. 60.

Robinson, J. D., "Key Player Chronicles Fascinating Search for AIDS Viruses," *Washington Post,* April 22, 1991, p. F1.

Specter, Michael, "The Case of Dr. Gallo," *New York Review of Books,* August 15, 1991, pp. 49–52.

Wade, Nicholas, "Method and Madness: The Vindication of Robert Gallo," *New York Times Magazine,* December 26, 1993, p. 12.

Harriet Hardy

Born September 23, 1905
Arlington, Massachusetts
Died October 13, 1993
Boston, Massachusetts

Harriet Hardy was a pioneer in the field of occupational medicine.

In the 1940s pathologist Harriet Louise Hardy investigated a respiratory illness that was common among factory workers in Massachusetts. (A pathologist is a doctor who studies the causes and effects of disease.) She discovered that workers were suffering from berylliosis, a sickness caused by exposure to beryllium (a toxic metal used in the manufacture of fluorescent lamps). Hardy ultimately became one of the world's leading authorities in the field of occupational medicine (the study of health hazards in the workplace). She devoted her career to researching many workplace hazards.

Begins studying industrial disease

Hardy was born on September 23, 1905, in Arlington, Massachusetts. In 1928 she graduated from Wellesley College in Massachusetts. Four years later she earned a medical degree from Cornell University in Ithaca, New York. After serving an internship and residency (two training programs for physicians) at Philadelphia General Hospital, Hardy was appointed school doctor at Northfield Seminary in Massachusetts. In 1939 she took a post as college doctor and director of health education at Radcliffe College in Cambridge, Massachusetts, where she began to study industrial diseases.

Investigates mysterious illness

In the early 1940s Hardy began a collaboration with Joseph Aubt to study the effects of lead poisoning on humans. (Lead poisoning is a condition caused by excessive levels of lead, a heavy metal, in tissues and blood.) Like occupational disease expert Alice Hamilton (see entry in volume four) and other pioneering pathologists, Hardy began to recognize the dangers that existed in the modern factory. Around this time she first heard about a strange respiratory disease among the workers in the Sylvania and General Electric fluorescent lamp factories in the nearby cities of Lynn and Salem, Massachusetts. The victims all complained of shortness of breath, coughing, and loss of weight. Some workers even died after exhibiting symptoms.

IMPACT

In the 1940s pathologist Harriet Hardy investigated an unusual pattern of sickness among workers at lamp factories in Massachusetts. She discovered that the workers were suffering from berylliosis, an illness caused by exposure to beryllium, a toxic metal used in the manufacture of fluorescent lamps. Hardy's investigation into berylliosis was one of the early successes in the field of occupational medicine. A respected scientist, Hardy devoted her career to researching many workplace hazards.

Finds source of disease

At first Hardy and her colleagues were baffled by the causes of the disease. Then Hardy realized there had to be a link to the workplaces of the patients. After reviewing research from Europe and Russia, she found a connection to beryllium. She learned that beryllium dust or vapor (mist that floats in the air) could have been easily inhaled by the factory workers. Hardy then determined that the outbreak in Massachusetts was indeed berylliosis, a condition in which symptoms sometimes do not appear for up to twenty years after exposure to beryllium.

Asbestos Linked to Cancer

In 1954 pathologist Harriet Hardy became one of the first scientists to identify asbestos, a mineral that separates into fibers, as a cancer-producing substance. Asbestos has since been linked with cancers of the larynx, kidneys, and intestines. It takes fifteen to thirty years to develop cancer after asbestos exposure. From 1900 through the early 1970s asbestos fibers were used in building materials as insulation for walls and pipes, fireproofing for walls and fireplaces, and for many other purposes. An asbestos health threat results only if the tiny fibers are released into the air, something that can happen with normal fraying or cracking of materials containing asbestos. Since the discovery of the link between asbestos and cancer, the U.S. government has passed laws requiring the removal of the hazardous substance from buildings and homes.

Hardy went on to become an expert in beryllium poisoning, writing papers that educated and alerted the medical community to its dangers. She also established a registry (detailed record) of berylliosis cases at the Massachusetts General Hospital in Boston, where she had been a member of the staff since 1940. This registry later served as a model for the tracking of other industrial diseases.

Founds occupational medicine clinic

In 1947 Hardy established a clinic of occupational medicine at Massachusetts General Hospital. Continuing her study of hazardous materials, in 1954 she was one of the first scientists to identify asbestos (a mineral that readily separates into fibers) as a carcinogen (a cancer-producing substance). She also studied the effects of radiation (energy in the form of waves or particles) on humans. Working with the federal Atomic Energy Commission in Los Alamos, New Mexico, she investigated radiation poisoning (a sickness resulting from exposure to radiation). Hardy initiated numerous improvements in working conditions in nuclear power plants. In 1949 she and Hamilton coauthored the second edition of *Industrial Toxicology,* the most authoritative reference book on radiation safety.

Other subjects of Hardy's research and investigation included mercury poisoning (a condition resulting from excessive levels of mercury in tissues and blood) and treatments for lead poisoning. Hardy also researched the harmful effects of benzene (a flammable hydrocarbon in liquid form). As a result of her findings, the highest concentration of benzene allowable in industrial processes was reduced by 50 percent.

Recognized as a leader

During the course of her long career, Hardy wrote more than one hundred scientific articles. She gained the respect of other scientists through her efforts to identify hazardous workplace materials and educate the scientific community about potential danger to workers. An outspoken and forceful advocate of change, Hardy was named Woman of the Year by the American Medical Women's Association in 1955. She reached another career milestone when she was appointed clinical professor at Harvard Medical School in Cambridge in 1971. Hardy died of lymphoma (cancer of the immune system) at age eighty-eight.

Further Reading

Harvard Medical School Focus, October 21, 1993, p. 9.

Journal of the American Medical Women's Association, November 1955, p. 402.

New York Times (obituary), October 15, 1993, p. B10.

Libbie Henrietta Hyman

Born December 6, 1888
Des Moines, Iowa
Died August 3, 1969

Libbie Henrietta Hyman produced influential work on the classification of invertebrate animals.

Libbie Henrietta Hyman earned an international reputation with *The Invertebrates,* her monumental six-volume work on the classification of invertebrates (animals without a spinal column). Although Hyman considered her project to be merely a compilation of existing literature on the subject, other scientists hailed it as a remarkable achievement. An independent woman with enormous knowledge and a talent for translating European languages, Hyman produced a wide-ranging summary of the invertebrate animal kingdom. Hyman's work had a lasting influence on scientific thinking about a number of invertebrate animal groups. She received several awards for her treatise, including the prestigious Gold Medal of the Linnaean Society.

Begins career in zoology

Hyman was born on December 6, 1888, in Des Moines, Iowa. She was the child of Jewish immigrants, Joseph Hyman

78

and Sabina Neumann. Hyman spent her childhood in Fort Dodge, Iowa, where her father kept an unsuccessful clothing store. Growing up in a strict home where affection was seldom expressed, Hyman became interested in nature at an early age. She learned the scientific names of flowers from a textbook on botany (the science of plants), and she collected butterflies and moths. In 1905 Hyman graduated as valedictorian (first in her class) from Fort Dodge High School. Five years later she earned a bachelor's degree in zoology (the study of animals) from the University of Chicago.

Hyman was then encouraged to enter the graduate program at the University of Chicago by Professor Charles Manning Child. When she became a graduate assistant to Child, Hyman's duties included directing laboratory work for courses in elementary zoology and comparative vertebrate anatomy (the study of animals with a spinal column). In 1915 Hyman earned a Ph.D., having written a dissertation entitled "An Analysis of the Process of Regeneration in Certain Micro-drilous Oligochaetes." She then became Child's research assistant. Among her duties was conducting physiological experiments on lower invertebrates. During this time she became a taxonomic specialist (a person who classifies animals) in invertebrate groups.

IMPACT

Zoologist Libbie Henrietta Hyman is best known for single-handedly compiling a six-volume landmark work on the classification of invertebrates. From translating foreign research articles to drawing illustrations, Hyman achieved a monumental feat in producing *The Invertebrates* (1931–1967)—a project that would normally be undertaken by a large group of scholars. Hyman's work brought new attention and clarity to the study of the invertebrate branch of the animal world. Hyman also influenced the teaching of zoology in America with the publication of her laboratory manuals.

Writes successful textbook

As Hyman helped conduct classes as a laboratory assistant, she saw the need for a better student guidebook. She decided to create such a text, and in 1919 *A Laboratory Manual for Elementary Zoology* was published by the University of Chicago Press. The first printing quickly sold out, and Hyman wrote an expanded edition ten years later. In 1922 she published *A Labo-*

Animal Regeneration

Libbie Henrietta Hyman wrote her doctoral dissertation on the subject of regeneration (the growth of new body parts) in certain animals. The process takes place mostly in less complex animal species, including primitive invertebrates. For example, a flatworm called a planarium can split symmetrically to become two identical worms. Among higher invertebrates, regeneration occurs in echinoderms such as starfish and in arthropods such as insects and crustaceans. Regeneration of limbs, wings, and antennae often takes place in cockroaches, fruit flies, lobsters, and crabs. On a very limited basis, some amphibians and reptiles can even replace a lost leg or tail.

ratory *Manual for Comparative Vertebrate Anatomy,* which also sold well. The second edition of this manual was published in 1942 as *Comparative Vertebrate Anatomy.* Hyman was never excited about vertebrates, however, and she refused to consider a third edition. (Published in 1979, the third edition was the work of eleven contributors.)

Publishes treatise on invertebrates

In 1931, after Hyman realized she could live on the royalties (percentage of profits) from the sale of her laboratory manuals, she left the University of Chicago. After traveling in Europe for fifteen months, she settled near the American Museum of Natural History in New York City. By this time Hyman was determined to devote her time to writing a complete and authoritative book on invertebrates. In 1937 she was made an honorary research associate at the museum. The first volume of *The Invertebrates* appeared three years later.

Hyman had always wanted to live in the country so that she could indulge her interest in gardening. In 1941 she bought a house in Millwood, Westchester County, about thirty-five miles north of New York City. Hyman commuted to the museum until 1952, when she sold the house and returned to the city. During her years in the country, she completed the second and third volumes of *The Invertebrates,* which were both published in 1951. At the museum, Hyman spent most of her time in the library. She read, made notes, digested information, mentally composed the text, and typed the first and only draft of her books on a manual (non-electric) typewriter. Hyman also taught herself drawing in order to create the illustrations for her books. She apparently never had a secretary or an assistant. The fourth volume of *The Invertebrates* was published in 1955 and the fifth volume was published in 1959.

Receives awards and honors

Active in many organizations, Hyman served as vice president of the American Society of Zoologists in 1953 and president of the Society of Systematic Zoology in 1959. She was a member of the National Academy of Sciences, the American Microscopical Society, and the American Society of Naturalists. In addition to her books, Hyman published 135 scientific papers between 1916 and 1966. In recognition of her work, the University of Chicago awarded Hyman an honorary doctorate in 1941. She also received the Daniel Giraud Elliot Medal of the National Academy of Sciences in 1951 and the Gold Medal of the Linnaean Society of London in 1960. In 1967 Hyman published the sixth and final volume of *The Invertebrates*. In April 1969 the American Museum presented her with its Gold Medal for Distinguished Achievement in Science. Hyman died four months later.

Further Reading

Hyman, Libbie Henrietta, and G. Evelyn Hutchinson, "Libbie Henrietta Hyman: December 6, 1888–August 3, 1969," *Biographical Memoirs,* National Academy of Sciences, Volume 60, 1991, pp. 103–14.

Rossiter, Margaret W., *Women Scientists in America: Struggles and Strategies to 1940,* Johns Hopkins University Press, 1982, pp. 210–11, 294, 373, 374.

Sicherman, Barbara, and Carol Hurd Green, eds. *Notable American Women: The Modern Period,* Belknap Press, 1980, pp. 365–67.

Stunkard, Horace W., "In Memoriam: Libbie Henrietta Hyman, 1888–1969," in *Biology of the Turbellaria,* edited by Nathan W. Riser and M. Patricia Morse, McGraw–Hill, 1974, pp. 9–13.

Winston, Judith E., "Great Invertebrate Zoologists: Libbie Henrietta Hyman (1888–1969)," *American Society of Zoologists, Division of Invertebrate Zoologists Newsletter,* fall 1991.

Hypatia of Alexandria

Born c. A.D. 370
Alexandria, Egypt
Died c. A.D. 415
Alexandria, Egypt

Hypatia of Alexandria was a famous female scholar and mathematician of the ancient world.

Portrait: Reproduced by permission of Corbis-Bettmann.

lthough all of her work has been lost or destroyed, historians regard Hypatia of Alexandria (an ancient city in Egypt) as the most famous female scholar of ancient times. She was the first woman ever known to teach and write about highly advanced mathematics. Letters by one of her students indicate that Hypatia, alone or with others, invented such mechanical instruments as the plane astrolabe and the hydrometer. Hypatia's fame is based not only on her legendary intellect, but also on her violent death. She was murdered by angry citizens of Alexandria during a time of political and religious tensions. After Hypatia was killed, the famous library of the Museum of Alexandria was burned and all of her writings were destroyed.

Absorbs spirit of learning

Hypatia was born in Alexandria around A.D. 370. She probably studied mathematics and astronomy (the observation of objects outside the Earth's atmosphere) with her father,

Theon of Alexandria. Theon was the last recorded member of the city's great museum. The Museum of Alexandria was a prominent cultural and intellectual center that resembled a large modern university. It consisted of several schools, public auditoriums, and the famous library, which housed one of the most comprehensive collections of books in the ancient world. Although the museum was in Egypt, its dominant culture was Greek. At one time scholars came from the Roman Empire, and even from as far away as Ethiopia and India. They heard lectures from noted scholars on the latest ideas and studied in the great library.

Because of Theon's connection with the museum (he may have been its director at one time), the institution was a major influence in Hypatia's life. As a child she spent much of her time at the museum and was exposed to a wide range of ideas. When she was ready to begin her formal studies, Hypatia was thoroughly educated in fields such as art, literature, science, and philosophy. Perhaps due to the influence of her father—who had an intense interest in mathematics—Hypatia concentrated on mathematics and philosophy. She traveled throughout the Mediterranean region to continue her studies. One of the places she visited was Athens, Greece, where she attended a school headed by Plutarch the Younger and his daughter, Asclepigenia. At this time Hypatia gained a reputation as a highly talented mathematician.

IMPACT

Hypatia of Alexandria was the most famous female scholar in the ancient world. Renowned as the best philosopher of her day, she was also a brilliant mathematician, energetic teacher, and thoughtful writer. Hypatia was a symbol of the great age of learning at the Museum of Alexandria. The museum was renowned for its huge library of ancient writings, which was eventually destroyed during a time of political upheaval. Hypatia wrote several mathematical and astronomical works, and with her father she coauthored critiques of works by Ptolemy and Euclid. She is also considered to have been partially responsible for the invention of the plane astrolabe and the hydrometer. Hypatia is probably best remembered for her death at the hands of a mob, an event that signaled the end of Alexandria's role as a great center of learning.

Attracts students and admirers

By the time Hypatia returned to Egypt, her abilities were so well known that she was invited to become a teacher at the

The Plane Astrolabe

Although written records are sketchy, it appears that Hypatia of Alexandria helped to invent the plane astrolabe. This instrument is a two-dimensional model of the heavens, with sights for observations. The astrolabe consists of two flat disks that are concentric, with one disk remaining fixed while the other is movable. The fixed disk represents the position of the observer on Earth. The moving disk can be rotated to represent the appearance of the celestial sphere at a given moment.

The plane astrolabe enables the observer to read the altitude and azimuth of any object in space. By measuring the altitude of a particular body, a person can calculate the time of day. The plane astrolabe can also be used to determine times of sunrise, sunset, and twilight. It was later replaced by the sextant, which is used for navigation, and other more accurate instruments.

Neoplatonic School in Alexandria. She was appointed director of the school in 400 A.D., when she was about thirty-one years old. Hypatia's lively lectures won her the admiration of students and scholars, many of whom traveled from great distances throughout the ancient world to study with her. Reports that have survived to the present day suggest that Hypatia was regarded as a greater philosopher than any men of her time. In addition, she was reputed to be a woman of unusual beauty and virtue. According to legend, Hypatia had many offers of marriage, but she refused her suitors by stating that she was "wedded to the truth."

Writes mathematical works

In addition to teaching, Hypatia wrote a number of books on mathematics and other subjects, including studies of philosophical and mathematical works by prominent scholars. It is believed that she assisted her father in a work of criticism on *Almagest* by the Greek mathematician and astronomer Ptolemy (see entry). In the book Ptolemy catalogued the stars and constellations and provided calculations of distances between objects in the solar system (the celestial bodies revolving around the Earth's sun). Hypatia and her father may also have been the authors of a revised version of *Elements,* a work on geometry and other mathematical concepts first proposed by Euclid (born c. 300 B.C.), the great Greek mathematician. (The father-daughter version of *Elements* was later used as the basis for modern editions of the work.) Hypatia wrote three books on her own, which were probably intended as textbooks for her students. One text was a collection of astronomical tables. The other books were commentaries on works by two Greek mathematicians, *Conic Sections* by Apollonius of Perga (c. 262 B.C.–c. 190 B.C.) and *Artithmetica* by Diophantus.

Helps invent devices

Hypatia corresponded with many distinguished scholars, some of whose letters have survived. Letters to Hypatia are often filled with praise for her talents and provide the few known details of her accomplishments. Although written records are sketchy, it appears that Hypatia invented or helped to invent mechanical devices such as the plane astrolabe (an instrument used by Greek astronomers to determine the position of the sun and stars). The plane astrolabe was probably developed with Synesius of Cyrene (c. A.D. 370–A.D. 413), a scholar who had attended Hypatia's classes and later became the Christian bishop of Ptolomais. In one letter to Hypatia, Synesius asks for advice on the construction of the instrument. He also worked with Hypatia on a hydrometer (a device used for measuring the weight of liquids) and a hydroscope (an instrument used to observe objects submerged in water).

An astrolabe. According to scholars, Hypatia invented—or helped to invent—mechanical devices such as the plane astrolabe, an instrument used by Greek astronomers to determine the position of the sun and stars. Reproduced by permission of AKG/Photo Researchers, Inc.

Murder signals end of era

When Hypatia was forty-five years old, she was brutally murdered by a group of Parabolans (fanatical Christian monks of the Church of St. Cyril). Reports of the event state that while Hypatia was on her way to the university, the monks dragged her from her chariot and tortured her to death. The motivations behind Hypatia's violent death have long been disputed, though her personal independence and pagan (non-Christian) beliefs seem to have created hostility among Alexandria's Christian community. Another contributing factor appears to have been Hypatia's alliance with Orestes, the governor of the city.

Hypatia of Alexandria

Orestes was also a pagan and a political adversary of Cyril (c. A.D. 375–A.D. 444), the Christian bishop of Alexandria. Hypatia's works were destroyed, along with many other records of ancient learning, when mobs burned the library of Alexandria and destroyed the entire collection. While a complete picture of Hypatia's contributions as a mathematician may never be achieved, it is apparent that she was a highly respected woman of her time. Her intellectual abilities and tragic death have made her a dramatic figure in scientific history.

Further Reading

Dictionary of Scientific Biography, Volume 6, Scribner's, 1972, pp. 615–16.

Ogilvie, Marilyn Bailey, *Women in Science: Antiquity through the Nineteenth Century,* MIT Press, 1986, pp. 104–5.

Osen, Lynn M., *Women in Mathematics,* MIT Press, 1974, pp. 21–32.

Sonya Vasilyevna Kovalevsky

Born January 15, 1850
Moscow, Russia
Died February 10, 1891
Stockholm, Sweden

Russian mathematician Sonya Vasilyevna Kovalevsky was a prominent nineteenth-century scholar. She is credited with developing an important mathematical theory known as the Cauchy-Kovalevsky theorem. Kovalevsky won great respect in her field, earning many prestigious prizes for her work; she was also one of the first women to become a professor of mathematics at the University of Stockholm in Sweden. Perhaps the greatest female mathematician prior to the twentieth century, Kovalevsky was also an accomplished playwright and novelist.

Sonya Vasilyevna Kovalevsky was a leading nineteenth-century Russian mathematician.

Wallpaper inspires math interest

Kovalevsky was born as Sonya Korvin-Krukovsky on January 15, 1850, in Moscow, Russia. She was the second of three children of Yelizaveta (Schubert) and Vasily Korvin-Krukovsky, a general in the Russian army. As a child Kovalevsky was educated by a Polish tutor who thought his

Portrait: Reproduced by permission of Corbis-Bettmann.

Russian mathematician Sonya Vasilyevna Kovalevsky was a great nineteenth-century scholar. Despite the challenges that prevented most women from reaching a high level of academic achievement, Kovalevsky studied with top mathematicians in Germany. Her doctoral dissertation developed an important mathematical theory that is today known as the Cauchy-Kovalevsky theorem. Not only did Kovalevsky complete a doctorate degree—a significant accomplishment for a woman at that time—she also became a noted professor at the University of Stockholm. In 1888 she won the coveted Prix Bordin of the French Academy of Sciences. Kovalevsky was perhaps the greatest female mathematician prior to the twentieth century.

young student had poor math skills. His judgment was surprising, considering the fact that Kovalevsky came from a long line of mathematicians that included her grandfather, Feodor Feodorovitch Schubert. Kovalevsky's uncle Piotr was perhaps her greatest influence in mathematics. Piotr had no formal training in the subject, but he loved to read and talk about math. Although young Sonya could not understand many of the concepts her uncle discussed, she was an attentive listener during their conversations.

When Kovalevsky was a child, an ordinary domestic situation helped to trigger her curiosity about mathematics. Her family once ordered wallpaper for the rooms in their house, but there was not enough to go around. As a temporary measure, the pages of a book on calculus belonging to Vasily Korvin-Krukovsky were used to cover the walls. Fascinated by the strange symbols on the pages, Kovalevsky would spend hours staring at the mysterious wall covering. These contemplations possibly gave her the ability to quickly absorb complex mathematical concepts. Eventually an instructor from St. Petersburg, Russia, discovered her talent and convinced her father to send her to school. Kovalevsky began studying mathematics in St. Petersburg when she was fifteen.

Absorbs new ideas

When Kovalevsky started school in St. Petersburg, the city was a center of intellectual activity and radical ideas. The young woman took part in the excitement that consumed educated Russians at the time. Along with her peers, she supported changes in society, especially advocating more freedom and opportunities for women. Women were not allowed to attend

Russian mathematician Sonya Vasilyevna Kovalevsky was a great scholar who encountered many obstacles during her lifetime because of her gender. In nineteenth-century Russia, women did not have control over their lives. Traditionally, decisions were made by their families or their husbands. Since women were not allowed to attend colleges and universities, their only alternative was to obtain private lessons from scholars. Sometimes classes were held for groups of women in private homes. Kovalevsky attended such gatherings and heard lectures by several notable academics, including the chemist Dmitry Mendeleev (see entry in volume two), the creator of the periodic table of elements (a chart that lists chemical elements according to number of atoms and atomic weight). She eventually became the first female professor at the University of Stockholm in Sweden.

colleges and universities, so they had to obtain private lessons from scholars. Because Kovalevsky was not satisfied with this type of informal education, she sought a way to continue her learning at a university where women would be accepted.

When Kovalevsky mentioned her wishes to her father, he scolded her for having such ideas. She realized her only option was to marry a man who was going to study in another country. In the fall of 1868, when she was eighteen, she married Vladimir Kovalevsky. The following spring the couple went to Heidelberg University in Germany, where Vladimir studied geology (a science that deals with the history of the earth). Sonya studied mathematics with Leo Königsberger and Emil Du Bois-Reymond. She took physics courses (the study of the interaction between energy and matter) from Gustav R. Kirchoff (1824–1887) and Herman L. F. von Helmholtz (1821–1894). Königsberger became one of her favorite teachers, and she studied with him for two years.

Develops influential theory

Königsberger had been a pupil of famous mathematician Karl T. Weierstrass (1815–1897). In 1871 Kovalevsky traveled to Germany to study with Weierstrass at the University of Berlin. Once she arrived, however, she discovered that the university did not admit women. Kovalevsky approached Weierstrass and asked him to accept her as a private student. Somewhat skeptical about her abilities, Weierstrass gave the young woman a test designed for advanced students. To his surprise, not only did she finish the problems quickly but her solutions showed considerable creativity and clear thinking. Impressed by her work, he spent the next four years tutoring Kovalevsky in the entire course of university mathematics.

Weierstrass was an important influence in Kovalevsky's career. While at Berlin, she published three mathematical papers that helped to establish her reputation as a talented mathematician. One dealt with abelian integers, a theory of natural numbers named for Norwegian mathematician Niels Abel (1802–1829). Another paper described the structure of the rings of the planet Saturn. The paper that became Kovalevsky's doctoral thesis, however, is considered her most important work. Titled "On the Theory of Partial Differential Equations," the document expanded the ideas of Augustan Louis Cauchy (1789–1857). Kovalevsky developed the theory into an even more generalized form, which is now known as the Cauchy-Kovalevsky theorem.

The high quality of Kovalevsky's work enabled her to qualify for the doctoral program at the University of Göttingen, the world-famous center for the study of mathematics and physics. After she received a degree in 1874, however, Kovalevsky had a difficult time finding a job because women were still not accepted as professors at any university in Europe. Ten years passed before she finally found a position in Sweden, where the social environment was more liberal than in other parts of Europe. In 1884 Kovalevsky was hired as a mathematics instructor at the University of Stockholm. She lectured on the latest and most advanced topics in mathematics, including inverse functions (operations, such as subtraction, that undo other operations), elliptical integrals (theories concerned with complex applications), and abelian functions.

Finally recognized in Russia

Kovalevsky flourished in Sweden, gaining a reputation as a brilliant teacher. She also created some of the best mathematical work of her life. One of her papers, "On the Problem of the Rotation of a Solid Body about a Fixed Point" (1888), earned the Prix Bordin of the French Academy of Sciences. The following year Kovalevsky's work on the same topic was honored with a prize from the Swedish Academy of Sciences. Because of her public success, Kovalevsky was granted a lifetime professorship at the University of Stockholm in 1889. That same year she was finally recognized in her native country when she was elected a member of the Russian Academy of Sciences.

In addition to her achievements in mathematics, Kovalevsky pursued a successful writing career. She wrote plays as well as several novels and autobiographical works. In 1887 her drama "The Struggle for Happiness" was performed to highly positive reviews. Kovalevsky's novels include *The Nihilist, The Sisters Raevsky,* and *A Story of the Riviera.* Kovalevsky's brilliant career was cut short when she died of pneumonia at the age of forty-one.

Further Reading

Dictionary of Scientific Biography, Volume 7, Scribner's, 1972, pp. 477–80.

Kovalevsky, Sonya Vasilyevna, *Recollections of Childhood,* translated by Isabel F. Hapgood, Century, 1895.

Ogilvie, Marilyn Bailey, *Women in Science: Antiquity through the Nineteenth Century,* MIT Press, 1986, pp. 133–39.

Osen, Lynn M., *Women in Mathematics,* MIT Press, 1974, pp. 117–40.

Rebecca Craighill Lancefield

Born January 5, 1895
Staten Island, New York
Died March 3, 1981

Rebecca Craighill Lancefield developed a system for classifying types of streptococcus bacteria.

Bacteriologist Rebecca Craighill Lancefield is known throughout the world for the system she developed to classify streptococcus bacteria (a group of disease-causing organisms). During a research career that spanned six decades, she identified more than fifty types of these bacteria. Lancefield used her knowledge of the large, diverse bacterial family to learn about the cause and development of diseases such as rheumatic fever (a condition that produces inflammation of the joints and heart). She also investigated the functioning of the immune system (the body's ability to resist infection). The Lancefield method of streptococcus classification has become a standard in medical science.

Investigates bacteria

Lancefield was born Rebecca Craighill on January 5, 1895, on Staten Island, New York. She was the third of six daughters of William Edward Craighill and Mary Montague

Byram. After changing her major from English to zoology (the scientific study of animal life), she received a bachelor's degree in 1916 from Wellesley College in Massachusetts. Two years later she earned a master's degree from Columbia University in New York City, where she studied bacteriology (the scientific study of bacteria) in the laboratory of American bacteriologist Hans Zinsser (1878–1940). Shortly after graduating from Columbia, she married classmate Donald Lancefield, with whom she later had a daughter.

Lancefield formed another lifelong partnership in 1918 when she began working at the Rockefeller Institute in New York City. She was hired to help bacteriologists Oswald Avery (c. 1887–1955) and Alphonse Dochez, who were experts on the pneumococcus bacterium, which causes pneumonia. At that time World War I (1914–1918) was in progress, and Avery and Dochez were pursuing a new area of investigation—a streptococcus epidemic that had broken out among soldiers in Texas. Using the soldiers' pneumococcus research as a basis, the scientists were trying to develop a serum (the part of blood that contains disease-fighting agents) that would prevent streptococcus infection. Within a year Avery, Dochez, and Lancefield had published a major report that described four types of streptococci. This report was Lancefield's first paper.

After the war the Lancefields took a short break from their work in New York City to teach at the University of Oregon. When the couple returned to New York City, Rebecca Lancefield began working on a Ph.D. at Columbia. During this time she also conducted studies on rheumatic fever at the Rockefeller Institute in the laboratory of researcher Homer Swift. Before World War I, physicians had suspected that a type of streptococcus caused rheumatic fever. But scientists, including Swift, had not been able to obtain a specific sample

IMPACT

Bacteriologist Rebecca Craighill Lancefield developed a method of classifying streptococcus bacteria. Known as the Lancefield system, this classification structure has become a standard in medical science. During the course of her career, Lancefield identified more than fifty varieties of the bacteria. By discovering components of streptococcus bacteria that cause illnesses in humans, Lancefield was better able to understand the functioning of the immune system and diseases such as rheumatic fever.

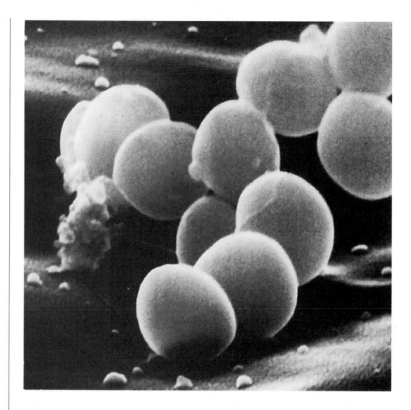

A staphylococcal bacteria infection under microscopic examination. Rebecca Craighill Lancefield used her knowledge of the bacterial family to learn about the cause and development of a variety of diseases. Reproduced by permission of Oliver Meckes. Photo Researchers, Inc.

of the bacterium from patients. Neither could they reproduce the disease in animals by using infected tissue from humans. Lancefield's first project with Swift, which also served as her doctoral research, showed that the alpha-hemolytic class of streptococcus was not the cause of rheumatic fever.

Classifies streptococci

As a result of working with Swift, Lancefield decided that a more basic approach to rheumatic fever was needed. She began sorting out types of disease-causing bacteria. Her major tool for classifying the bacteria was the precipitin test. This procedure involved mixing specific antigens (substances that stimulate immune responses) with antisera (types of serum containing antibodies) to separate bacteria from the liquid in the serum. Once the bacteria were isolated in this way, they could be studied more closely.

Lancefield soon recovered two antigens from the streptococci. One antigen was a polysaccharide (a carbohydrate) called the C substance. This complex sugar molecule is a major component of the cell wall in all streptococci. As Lancefield discovered other carbohydrate antigens, she grouped the bacteria according to which type of antigen they possessed, labeling the groups with the letters *A* through *O*. In group A she placed the streptococci that most commonly cause human disease. Among the group A streptococci Lancefield found another antigen. She determined it was a protein (a naturally occurring substance in cells), which she called *M* because of its matte (dull) appearance. By identifying differences in M protein composition, Lancefield was then able to subdivide group A streptococci into a number of more specific types.

Describes M antigen

In further studies of the M protein, Lancefield revealed that this antigen is responsible for the virulence (strong disease-causing abilities) of streptococci. The M protein keeps white blood cells, which are the body's normal defense against infection, from surrounding and destroying the streptococci. This finding came as a surprise, because Avery had discovered that virulence in the pneumococcus was due to a polysaccharide, not a protein. Lancefield went on to show the M antigen is also responsible for creating protective immune reactions.

Researches disease and immunity

Once her system of classification was in place, Lancefield returned to her original quest. She explored the connections between substances in bacteria and the baffling nature of streptococcal diseases. Among the most common of these diseases are sore throat, rheumatic fever, scarlet fever (a disease of the nose, throat, and mouth), and infections of the heart and kidneys. She found that a single type of group A streptococcus can cause a variety of diseases. This evidence reversed a long-standing belief that every disease must be caused by a specific microbe (a tiny organism). Lancefield also found that acquired

Rebecca Craighill Lancefield

Pioneers Meningitis Treatment

Late in her career, bacteriologist Rebecca Craighill Lancefield focused on antigen studies. Ten years after her official retirement, she made a vital contribution to the understanding of the group B streptococci. Lancefield clarified the role of polysaccharides in virulence, showing how antigens on the surface of polysaccharides also play a protective role in fighting disease. During the 1970s, when an increasing number of infants were being born with group B meningitis, her work laid the basis for the medical response to this problem.

immunity (the ability to resist disease that occurs through repeated exposure) to one group A streptococcus could not protect against infections caused by streptococci in group A.

From her laboratory at Rockefeller Hospital in New York City, Lancefield could follow patient records for long periods of time. Her study determined that once immunity to a type of streptococcus is acquired, it can last up to thirty years. Lancefield's work further revealed that high concentrations of antibodies (proteins produced in an immune response) continue to exist even when the antigen is no longer present. In the case of rheumatic fever, Lancefield illustrated that a patient can suffer several attacks of the disease because each attack is caused by a different type of streptococcus bacterium.

Honored late in career

Throughout a long career Lancefield continued to describe and categorize streptococcus organisms sent from laboratories around the world. Until the end of her life, her painstaking investigations helped unravel the complexity and diversity of these bacteria. During World War II (1939–1945), Lancefield performed special duties for the Streptococcal Diseases Commission of the Armed Forces Epidemiological Board. In 1946 she became an associate member at Rockefeller, being promoted to full member and professor in 1958 and emerita professor (an honorary title) in 1965.

Despite Lancefield's numerous achievements, full recognition of her work did not come until shortly before she retired. In 1961 she became the first woman to be elected president of the American Association of Immunologists, and in 1970 she was one of the few women elected to the National Academy of Sciences. Other honors included the T. Duckett

Jones Memorial Award in 1960, the American Heart Association Achievement Award in 1964, the New York Academy of Medicine Medal in 1973, and honorary degrees from Rockefeller University in 1973 and Wellesley College in 1976. Remaining active until the end of her life, Lancefield died of complications from a hip injury at the age of eighty-six. Her husband followed her in death three months later.

Further Reading

McCarty, M., "Rebecca Craighill Lancefield," *Biographical Memoirs: National Academy of Sciences,* Volume 57, 1987, pp. 226–46.

O'Hern, E. M., *Profiles of Pioneer Women Scientists,* Acropolis Books, 1985, pp. 69–78.

Schwartz, J. N., "Mrs. L.," *Research Profiles,* summer 1990, pp. 1–6.

Wannamaker, L., "Rebecca Craighill Lancefield," *American Society for Microbiology News,* Volume 47, 1981, pp. 555–58.

Inge Lehmann

Born May 13, 1888
Copenhagen, Denmark
Died 1993
Denmark

Inge Lehmann discovered the solid core at the center of the Earth.

Inge Lehmann was a famous Danish geophysicist (a scientist who studies the Earth). She was initially trained as a mathematician and actuary (a person who calculates statistics for life insurance companies). Using her background in statistics, Lehmann carefully kept records of observations and measurements of shock waves generated by earthquakes. In 1936 she proposed that the Earth has a solid inner core. Throughout her long career, which extended far beyond her official retirement in 1953, Lehmann conducted research in Europe and North America. She was also active in international scientific organizations. One of her most important affiliations was with the European Seismological Federation, which she cofounded and served as its first president.

Begins career as actuary

Lehmann was born on May 13, 1888, one of two daughters of Alfred Georg Ludvig Lehmann and Ida Sophie Torsleff.

As a child Lehmann graduated from the first school in Denmark to admit both girls and boys. The institution was founded and run by Hanna Adler, the aunt of Nobel Prize-winning physicist Niels Bohr (see entry). Lehmann began her education in mathematics at the University of Copenhagen from 1907 to 1910. She continued her studies the following year at Cambridge University in England before returning to Denmark, where she worked as an actuary from 1912 to 1918.

Helps install seismographs

Deciding to change careers, Lehmann earned a master's degree in mathematics from the University of Copenhagen in 1920 and continued her studies at the University of Hamburg in Germany. In 1925 she became a seismologist (a scientist who studies earthquakes) at the Royal Danish Geodetic Institute in Copenhagen, where she helped install the first seismographs (machines that measure vibrations of the Earth) in Denmark. Lehmann was so inspired by the capabilities of the seismograph that she later helped establish other seismograph stations in Denmark and Greenland.

Heads institute

Lehmann pursued her interest in the internal structure of the Earth by studying with seismologists in France, Germany, Belgium, and the Netherlands. After earning a master of science degree in geodesy (a branch of mathematics concerned with the size and shape of the Earth) from the University of Copenhagen in 1928, Lehmann was named chief of the Royal Danish Geodetic Institute. In that position, which she held until her retirement in 1953, she worked as the only seismologist in Denmark for more than two decades. She was responsi-

IMPACT

Inge Lehmann was a mathematician and geophysicist who single-handedly oversaw the seismology program in Denmark for more than twenty years. During this time she focused her attention on earthquakes occurring in the Pacific Ocean and observed the types of waves produced by the quakes. In 1936 Lehmann's studies led her to conclude that the Earth must have a small, solid core. This theory was later proven correct by other scientists. For her achievements in geophysics, Lehmann was awarded the William Bowie Medal of the American Geophysical Union in 1971.

The Structure of the Earth

The earth is divided into a number of layers. The topmost layer is the crust, which consists of granite and basalt. The depth of the crust ranges from five miles to fifty miles (approximately eight kilometers to eighty kilometers). Beneath the crust is a boundary known as the Moho discontinuity, named after Croatian geophysicist Andrija Mohorovicic (1857–1936). Below the Moho is the mantle, a mostly solid layer consisting of minerals and gas, which extends down about 1,800 miles (around 2,900 kilometers).

Even though seismologist Inge Lehmann hypothesized the existence of a core at the center of the Earth, this area is named after German-born American seismologist Beno Gutenburg. Known as the Gutenburg discontinuity, the liquid outer core extends from the base of the mantle down 3,200 miles (about 5,155 kilometers). The solid inner core reaches from the bottom of the outer core to the center of the Earth, about 3,956 miles (around 6,371 kilometers). The temperature of the inner core is estimated to be about 7,000 degrees Fahrenheit (3,850 degrees Celsius).

ble for supervising the national seismology program, overseeing the operation of seismograph stations in Denmark and Greenland, and preparing the institute's bulletins.

Discovers inner core of Earth

Despite the time-consuming job of running the Geodetic Institute, Lehmann managed to conduct extensive scientific research. In 1936 she published her most significant finding, the discovery of the Earth's inner core, under the simple title of "P." The letter P stood for the three types of waves generated by earthquakes under the Pacific Ocean, which Lehmann had been carefully observing for ten years. By studying the shock waves that were generated by earthquakes and then recorded on the seismographs, she theorized that the Earth has a smaller solid inner core. Within a few years Lehmann's work was confirmed by English geophysicist Harold Jeffreys (1891–1989) and German-born American seismologist Beno Gutenberg (1889–1960).

Recognized by scientific community

Lehmann continued her research well after her retirement in 1953, studying at various locations in Denmark, Canada, and the United States. She was held in high esteem by the scientific community for her research on the structure and internal activities of the Earth. In 1971 she was awarded the William Bowie Medal of the American Geophysical Union in recognition for her outstanding work. She was also awarded honorary doctorates by the University of Copenhagen and Columbia University in New York City. Lehmann, who was also a great humanitarian, lived a long and active life. She died in 1993 at the age of 105.

Further Reading

Bolt, Bruce A., *Inside the Earth,* W. H. Freeman, 1982, pp. 18–21.

EOS Transactions, American Geophysical Union, July 1971, pp. 537–38.

Journal of Geological Education, Volume 30, 1982, pp. 291–92.

Rossbacher, Lisa A., "The Geologic Column," *Geotimes,* August 1993, p. 36.

Gottfried Wilhelm Leibniz

Born July 1, 1646
Leipzig, Saxony, Germany
Died November 16, 1716
Hanover, Germany

Gottfried Wilhelm Leibniz is credited with the creation of differential calculus.

Gottfried Wilhelm Leibniz has been called the "Aristotle of the seventeenth century" because of his contributions to science and philosophy. Best known during his life as a royal councillor (adviser) and diplomat, he is now remembered for his contributions to mathematics and philosophy. Among his achievements were a system of notation for calculus (a method of using notations to perform computations), demonstration of the importance of binary numbers (numbers having 2 as a base) and symbolic (now known as Boolean) logic, and the development of a calculating machine. Although Leibniz died in obscurity, he is regarded as one of the great figures of the Enlightenment. (The Enlightenment was a philosophical movement during the eighteenth century that was marked by rejection of traditional social, religious, and political ideas in favor of rationalism.)

Child prodigy

Leibniz was born on July 1 (some sources say June 23), 1646, in Leipzig, Germany. His mother, Katherina Schmuck, came from an academic family and his father, Friedrich Leibniz, was a professor of philosophy at the University of Leipzig. Although Friedrich died when Leibniz was only six years old, his extensive library of historical and classical literature significantly influenced his son's intellectual development. The young Leibniz had an insatiable appetite for reading, and he spent most of his time in the library. Educated primarily at home, Leibniz soon proved himself to be a prodigy (a highly talented child). By the age of eight he had taught himself Latin; by the time he was fourteen, he had mastered the Greek language. Leibniz's interest in almost every subject he encountered, as well as his love of reading, continued throughout his life.

At the age of fifteen Leibniz entered the University of Leipzig to study law in preparation for a political career. He also studied theology (religious faith, practice, and experience), philosophy, and mathematics. After receiving a bachelor's degree in 1663, he briefly remained at Leipzig. Then he transferred to the University of Altdorf, where he earned a doctorate in law in 1666. Although Leibniz was invited to stay at Altdorf as a professor, he declined the offer in order to enter politics.

In 1669 Leibniz obtained a position in the service of Johann Philipp von Schöborn (1605–1673), the elector (prince of the Holy Roman Empire) of Mainz, Germany. For the next six years Leibniz composed official documents and correspondence for the elector and participated in diplomatic missions to France and England. During this time he also worked on various issues in mathematics, an interest he had begun to develop

IMPACT

Gottfried Wilhelm Leibniz made several contributions to mathematics during the seventeenth century. His work led to modern advances in the fields of computer theory and cybernetics. Leibniz was the first person to propose that logical thought could be reduced to mathematical operations. During the nineteenth and twentieth centuries his theory was developed into a system now known as Boolean algebra. Leibniz also discovered the usefulness of the Chinese binary number system. His predictions were realized during the twentieth century with the use of the binary system in the programming of digital computers.

Christian Huygens: A Great Influence

Gottfried Wilhelm Leibniz was a successful diplomat as well as one of the foremost mathematicians of the eighteenth century. During a diplomatic mission to Paris, France, in 1672 Leibniz met Christian Huygens (1629–1695), the famous Dutch mathematician, physicist, and astronomer. The two men formed a lifelong friendship. Discussions with Huygens inspired Leibniz to intensify his investigation of mathematical theories, which became the basis of much of his later scientific work. Leibniz's goal was to bring logical order to the entire realm of science. To do this, Leibniz planned to create a universal scientific language and a "calculus of reasoning." These ambitious ideas were years ahead of their time.

in college. Leibniz published his first paper on mathematics in 1666. Entitled *De arte combinatorica,* the paper expressed Leibniz's belief that logical thought processes could be reduced to mathematical combinations. These concepts were put to use during the twentieth century in the development of Boolean algebra and the programming of digital computers (computers that operate with numbers expressed directly as digits).

Improves calculating machine

While studying mathematics, Leibniz became intrigued with finding a way to reduce the amount of time and tedium involved in making calculations in astronomy (observations of celestial bodies) and navigation (charting of ocean and sea routes). His solution was to create a calculator (a mechanical device for performing mathematical calculations). He studied an earlier calculator, designed by French mathematician Blaise Pascal (1623–1662), which could only add and subtract. Leibniz worked to produce a design that could perform multiplication and division. In 1671 Leibniz introduced his calculator, which turned out to be a success. After he demonstrated the machine for the Royal Society in London, England, in 1673, he was elected a member of the scientific organization. Leibniz's innovations included multiplier wheels and other features that would be used in calculators for the next three hundred years. The original machine Leibniz built is preserved in the State Library in Hanover, Germany.

Makes contributions to calculus

After Schöborn's death in 1673, Leibniz was not retained as court councillor. He returned to Paris, where he began working on one of his most important contributions to mathematics—a system of integral and differential calculus. (Integral calculus involves combining mathematical procedures. Differential calculus is concerned with the rate of change of mathematical functions.) He published his theory the following year. Although the English mathematician and physicist Isaac Newton (see entry in volume four) was conducting similar studies, there is no evidence that either man was aware of the other's work. At the time, however, most mathematicians considered Leibniz's notations to be superior to those compiled by Newton. As a result, a bitter controversy erupted between the two scientists. In a debate that lasted nearly ten years, Leibniz was charged with plagiarizing (misrepresenting as his own) Newton's work. The accusations were eventually proven false. Yet the argument resulted in a decline in Leibniz's popularity, particularly among the English, who stubbornly continued to use Newton's system.

Promotes binary numbers

In 1676 Leibniz returned to Germany. He was then appointed adviser and librarian to Johann Friedrich, the duke of Brunswick-Lüneburg, in Hanover. When Friedrich died in 1679, Leibniz became a councillor at court. One of his projects was to trace the Brunswick family tree (a tree-like diagram that lists ancestors and their descendents), a task that involved numerous trips abroad. During his travels Leibniz met many prominent European scientists. In 1679 he began studying the use of binary numbers. Tracing the concept back to eleventh-century China, Leibniz became the first to recognize the importance of binary numbers. Nevertheless, practical application of the system in the Western world did not occur until 250 years later, when scientists began using binary numbers to program digital computers.

Later work and writing

Leibniz continued to hold diplomatic positions, including councillor to the royal courts of Russia and Austria. He also

became interested in a wide range of fields, including geology, psychology, philosophy, and history. In 1678 he founded the popular journal *Acta eruditorum,* in which many of his own papers were published. Five years later he introduced a statement of the law of conservation of mechanical energy. (The law of conservation of energy states that the total energy of an isolated system remains constant in spite of internal changes.) This concept was eventually developed to explain the conservation of all types of energy.

Another of Leibniz's contributions was the aneroid barometer (a device that uses a thin piece of metal instead of a column of mercury to measure air pressure). In a paper titled *Protogea,* which was published after his death, Leibniz explained his theory of the development of the Earth. According to Leibniz, the Earth began as vapor, then changed to a molten globular state, and finally evolved into its present form. In addition, he accounted for geological irregularities in the Earth's crust, concepts that were eventually confirmed by geologists.

Builds academy

In 1700 Leibniz founded the Berlin Academy of Sciences. Explaining the need to compete with scientists in London and Paris, Leibniz persuaded Prince Frederick of Prussia (1688–1740; later King Frederick I) to build the institution. Leibniz was the Academy's first president, holding the position until his death.

Although Leibniz had made numerous scientific advances and enjoyed a successful diplomatic career, he spent his final years in relative obscurity. After George I (1660–1727) became king of England, Leibniz asked for a position in the court. George rejected this request, possibly because of the controversy between Leibniz and Newton. By the time Leibniz died in 1716, many people in the scientific and mathematical communities had forgotten him. He neither married nor had a family, and the only mourner at his funeral was his secretary. An eyewitness wrote, "[Leibniz] was buried more like a robber than what he really was, the ornament of his country." While Leibniz's contemporaries may have overlooked his innovative studies, future generations recognized the genius of his work and the importance of his contributions.

Further Reading

Asimov, Isaac, *Asimov's Biographical Encyclopedia of Science and Technology,* rev. ed., Doubleday, 1972, pp. 142–43.

Dictionary of Scientific Biography, Volume 8, Scribner's, 1972, pp. 149–68.

McGraw-Hill Encyclopedia of World Biography, Volume 6, McGraw-Hill, 1973, pp. 408–11.

Georges Lemaître

Born July 17, 1894
Charleroi, Belgium
Died June 20, 1966
Louvain, Belgium

Georges Lemaître was the primary author of the big bang theory of the creation of the universe.

Georges Edouard Lemaître was both a Roman Catholic priest and mathematical physicist. He became one of the first scientists to suggest the big bang theory of the creation and evolution of the universe. Lemaître based his idea on the belief that if galaxies (large groups of stars) in the universe are now moving away from each other, they must have been closer together at one time. He proposed that all matter in the universe was once contained in a "primeval atom" before being scattered, and radically changed, by a massive explosion. The big bang theory has been called the greatest achievement of modern cosmology (a branch of astronomy that deals with the structure of the universe).

Studies physics and mathematics

Lemaître was born on July 17, 1894, in Charleroi, Belgium, into a deeply religious family. His father was Joseph Lemaître, a lawyer, and his mother was Marguerite Lannoy

Lemaître. Believing that he could find truth in both religion and science, Lemaître decided to become a Roman Catholic priest and a scientist. In 1914 he graduated as a mining engineer from the University of Louvain, in Belgium. While serving in the Belgian Army during World War I (1914–1918), Lemaître read *Electricite et optique* ("Electricity and Optics") by French mathematician Jules-Henri Poincaré (1854–1912). Poincaré's book prompted Lemaître to reconsider his career as an engineer. After the war he returned to Louvain to study physics (the science of the relationship between energy and matter) and mathematics, receiving a master's degree in 1920.

After briefly working toward a doctorate, Lemaître entered the seminary (an institution that trains priests) at Mailines, Belgium, in 1920. He was ordained (officially appointed) as a Roman Catholic priest three years later. Lemaître then received several fellowships that enabled him to go abroad to pursue a doctorate degree. In 1924 he studied solar physics (the science pertaining to the energy of the Sun) at Cambridge University in England,

IMPACT

Mathematical physicist Georges Lemaître led a revolution in science. He proposed that the universe once existed in a small, dense body, which exploded in a single event that is now called the "big bang." This powerful explosion is thought to have been the force that created the universe. The idea met with skepticism when it first appeared in the late 1920s. The big bang theory gained acceptance in the 1960s, however, on the basis of evidence provided by the radio telescope. While some of Lemaître's concepts have been modified by other scientists, the big bang theory remains the most widely accepted explanation of the creation of the universe.

where he worked with English astronomer Arthur Eddington (1882–1944). The following year Lemaître went to Cambridge, Massachusetts, and studied at Harvard University and the Massachusetts Institute of Technology (MIT). He focused his research on the theory of relativity, which was developed by physicist Albert Einstein (see entry in volume one). (The theory of relativity states the relationship between measurements taken on two systems that are moving with respect to each other.) After receiving a doctorate from MIT in 1927, Lemaître returned to the University of Louvain.

During his time in England and the United States, Lemaître met and worked with some of the world's greatest astronomers. Besides Eddington, he became acquainted with American astronomers Edwin Hubble (see entry in volume two), Harlow Shapley (1885–1972), and Vesto M. Slipher (1875–1969). Since 1912 Slipher had been measuring the radial velocities of galaxies (the speed at wlich galaxies are moving toward or away from the Earth along a line of sight). Slipher found that most galaxies seemed to be moving away from the Milky Way. Hubble, too, observed that galaxies were moving away from each other. In 1929 he formulated Hubble's law, which states that the distance to a galaxy and the velocity at which it is moving away are directly related. Like Hubble, Shapley had worked at Mount Wilson Observatory in California, where he determined the size of the Milky Way and the position of the Sun within it. These advances in astronomy contributed to Lemaître's examination of the theory of relativity.

Formulates big bang theory

One of the components of Einstein's original theory of relativity was the proposition that the universe is static (unchanging), yet it could collapse if disturbed. Einstein based this idea on a series of mathematical calculations, which he later retracted because he considered them the biggest mistake of his career. Before Einstein realized his error, however, Lemaître had already begun to question the idea of a static universe, partly on the basis of what he had learned from the observations of American and English astronomers. In 1927 Lemaître published a paper entitled "A Homogeneous Universe of Constant Mass and Increasing Radiation, Taking Account of the Radial Velocity of Extragalactic Nebulae." He argued that if all the galaxies in the universe were speeding away from each other, they had to have been closer together at some point in the past. Lemaître envisioned the matter and energy of the universe to have been wrapped up tightly in what he called a primeval atom. He pictured this atom, which resembled an egg, to be about thirty times the size of the Sun and so dense that it could not be measured.

Lemaître believed that between twenty and sixty billion years ago, the primal atom burst in an explosion, throwing

matter and energy off in all directions. This explosion caused an expansion of the universe that continued until the universe had gained a width of about one billion light-years. (A light-year is the distance that light travels in one year in a vacuum, about 5.88 trillion miles or 9.46 trillion kilometers.) To explain this expansion, Lemaître postulated the existence of what he called cosmical repulsion (an opposite force to gravity). He speculated that cosmical repulsion grew stronger as objects became more distant from each other, thus continuing the expansion of the universe. Lemaître also believed that, as a result of the big bang explosion, the original density (concentration) of matter had been reduced so greatly that atoms like hydrogen (the simplest element) had been able to form larger, more complex atoms.

Lemaître did not realize that five years earlier, Russian meteorologist and mathematician Aleksandr Friedmann (1888–1925) had challenged Einstein's assumption of a static universe. Pointing out that Einstein had made an error in the calculations he used to devise his theory, Friedmann reached essentially the same conclusion as Lemaître about the origins of the universe. The work of Friedmann and Lemaître, who are now considered cofounders of the big bang theory, greatly simplified the calculations needed for the theory of relativity.

Theory refuted, then accepted

In 1932, when Lemaître explained the big bang theory in a lecture at Mount Wilson Observatory, he was praised by scientists such as Einstein. Nevertheless, his idea lacked sufficient mathematical backing for widespread acceptance. Even the discovery of cosmic rays (streams of atomic nuclei that travel through space at the speed of light), in the early 1930s, did not make his theory more acceptable. Finally, in 1946, when American physicist George Gamow (1904–1968) provided mathematical backing for Lemaître's work, scientists began to take the theory seriously. Gamow examined the big bang from the time immediately before it began, in theory, to just after it ended. He abandoned Lemaître's idea of cosmical repulsion and argued that the force of the initial explosion alone would have been enough to cause the universe to continue to expand.

Even though the big bang theory had been proven mathematically, scientists still disagreed with it. In 1948 Austrian-born English mathematician Hermann Bondi (1919–) and Austrian-born American astronomer Thomas Gold (1920–) who were working at Cambridge University, suggested that there had never been a big bang. Bondi and Gold argued for what came to be known as the steady state theory (the assertion that the universe has always existed and has never changed). They believed that as galaxies moved out of range of observation, new galaxies formed in the spaces in between. Therefore the number of visible galaxies remained fairly constant. Among the steady state supporters was the astronomer Fred Hoyle (see entry in volume five), who refined and popularized the theory.

Advocates of the big bang and steady state theories remained rivals throughout the 1950s and 1960s. Results from the use of the radio telescope (a device that gathers radio signals from space), however, eventually disproved the steady state theory. With the aid of the radio telescope scientists discovered that because light takes so long to travel through space, astronomers on earth are actually studying light from stars as they existed thousands of millions of years ago. English astronomer Sir Martin Ryle (1918–1984) at Cambridge University showed that the distribution of distant galaxies is not the same as that of galaxies closer to the earth in space and time. Ryle thus proved the universe is constantly changing. In 1965 astronomers presented strong evidence that there had been a period of time when the universe was hot and dense, as it would have been immediately after the big bang. Even though scientists continue to pose other theories about the creation of the universe, modified versions of Lemaître's theory are still the most widely accepted.

Receives awards and honors

After 1927 Lemaître became a professor of astrophysics at the University of Louvain. Throughout his career he continued to refine the big bang theory and to investigate such subjects as the three-body problem (the way in which three celestial bodies, such as planets, act on each other). He also remained active in the Roman Catholic Church, never acknowledging a conflict between his scientific work and his religious beliefs. Lemaître was awarded the Prix Francqui in 1934. The following year Villanova University presented him with the Mendel Medal, and he received an

Radio Astronomy

As a result of the invention of the radio telescope, the big bang theory, which was formulated by physicist Georges Lemaître, has gained acceptance. Radio astronomy began in the 1930s when American engineer Karl Jansky (1905–1950) built a radio receiver designed to locate interference that was plaguing long distance telephone lines. When interference was proven to be coming from the Milky Way, the Earth's galaxy, scientists realized they could use radio telescopes to map the universe. In 1955 English astronomer Sir Martin Ryle (1918–1984) invented radio interferometry, which uses several small radio telescopes to create a huge instrument called a dish. In 1964 Ryle placed three radio telescopes one mile apart, forming the equivalent of a single dish of the same diameter. In the 1970s, the National Radio Astronomy Observatory (NRAO) built the Very Large Array (VLA) radio interferometer in New Mexico. The VLA is currently the largest radio telescope in the world.

honorary degree from McGill University. Shortly before his death Lemaître became president of the Pontifical Academy of Sciences in Rome, Italy.

Further Reading

Aikman, Duncan, "Lemaître Follows Two Paths to Truth," *New York Times Magazine,* February 19, 1933, pp. 3, 18.

Cevasco, George A., "The Universe and Abbé Lemaître," *Catholic World,* June 1951, pp. 184–88.

"Earth's Age Given as Two Billion Years," *New York Times,* July 24, 1933, p. 16.

"Finds No Conflict of Science, Religion," *New York Times,* December 11, 1932.

Gamow, George, *The Creation of the Universe,* Viking, 1961.

Hartmann, William K., *Astronomy: The Cosmic Journey,* Wadsworth, 1987.

Jastrow, Robert, *God and the Astronomers,* Norton, 1978.

Moore, Patrick, *The History of Astronomy,* Oldbourne, 1983.

Physics Today, September 1966, pp. 119–20.

Rival Theories of Cosmology, Oxford University Press, 1960.

Silk, James, *The Big Bang,* W. H. Freeman, 1980, pp. 20–26.

Estella Bergere Leopold

Born January 8, 1927
Madison, Wisconsin

E stella Bergere Leopold has never seen most of the plants she studies because they died millions of years ago. Yet Leopold has discovered what they looked like, how they were nourished, and how they reproduced. She reached her conclusions by looking at fossils (traces of organisms from past geologic ages) of plant spores, seeds, and leaves. Leopold is known as one of the leading authorities on paleoecology (the study of prehistoric organisms and their environments). When interviewed for an article in *Notable Twentieth-Century Scientists,* Leopold explained her work: "We compare assemblages of pollen and spores as they appear on the landscape today with those we find in rocks for a particular time period, and try to get the idea of the landscape and climate represented by the fossils. The fossils are probably the most important evidence of environments of the past. You put all this together and get a picture of past landscapes."

Estella Bergere Leopold is a leading authority on paleoecology, the study of prehistoric organisms and environments.

Paleoecologist Estella Bergere Leopold has spent her career studying forces that influenced habitats and organisms that lived on Earth millions of years ago. By analyzing fossils of the leaves and seeds of ancient plants, she has been able to trace evolutionary changes in forests in the Rocky Mountains in Colorado and other areas. One of her most important findings is that in places where climate changes are greatest, evolution has been more dynamic and extinctions have been more frequent. The daughter of renowned conservationist Aldo Leopold, she has also been active in preserving and restoring natural habitats in the modern world.

Shares family love of nature

Since childhood, Leopold has been studying landscapes in order to recreate their history. She was born on January 8, 1927, in Madison, Wisconsin. Her most cherished memories, however, are of weekends on the family farm fifty miles north of her home. There, the young scientist was taught how to "read signs" of wildlife by her father, famous writer and conservationist Aldo Leopold (see entry in volume five). The elder Leopold preserved his memories of the farm for generations of naturalists in his popular book, *A Sand County Almanac* (1949).

Aldo Leopold also taught his children the value of conservation (the management of natural resources). The family spent much of its time at the farm planting tree seedlings and restoring an old cornfield to its original state as a tall-grass prairie. Leopold's mother, Estella Bergere Leopold, was a homemaker who shared her husband's love of the outdoors. All five of the Leopold children pursued careers in science.

In 1948 Leopold earned a bachelor's degree in botany at the University of Wisconsin at Madison, where her father had taught wildlife management. Two years later she received a master's degree in botany from the University of California at Berkeley. Although Leopold had been accepted into the doctoral program at the University of California at Los Angeles (UCLA), she changed her plans when she heard that UCLA professors were particularly hard on female students. A colleague persuaded her to study at Yale University in New Haven, Connecticut, where she was welcomed by English-born American ecologist George Evelyn Hutchinson (1903–1991) and other acclaimed ecologists.

Leopold was the only female graduate studying science, yet she felt comfortable at Yale. While investigating ice-age environments in Connecticut, the young botanist developed her interest in paleoecology. Leopold earned a Ph.D. in 1955. Her dream was to teach but, feeling intimidated by male competition, she settled for the security of government work.

Discovers evolutionary patterns

Leopold had a long and distinguished career as a research paleobiologist for the U.S. Geological Survey in Denver, Colorado. During her work with the Geological Survey, she dug into the layers of earth and rock in the Rocky Mountains to reconstruct the evolution (gradual change over time) of forests over sixty million years. Her research revealed that patterns of evolution were influenced by changes in landscape and climate (the average weather conditions in an area). Leopold concluded that extinction (the disappearance of species) and evolutionary changes have been highest in the middle of the continent, where seasonal climate fluctuations are greatest. Coastal areas, which have more moderate climates, are able to sustain older species, such as the giant redwood tree (a commercially important coniferous timber tree).

Receives awards and honors

In 1967 Leopold finally realized her dream of becoming a teacher when she was appointed professor at the University of Colorado. After retiring from the U.S. Geological Survey in 1976, she continued her career as head of the Quaternary Research Center at the University of Washington. She left that post in 1982 to become a professor at the university.

Leopold has received several awards and honors for her work. She was named Conservationist of the Year by the Col-

A Family Tradition

Paleoecologist Estella Bergere Leopold comes from a family of scientists. Her father, Aldo Leopold, was a famous American environmentalist. Her brother, Luna Leopold (1915–), is a leading authority on hydrology. After he began working for the U.S. Geological Survey in 1950, he developed a theory about the hydraulics of river flow. At that time scientists believed the path of a river was determined by its sediment load. Leopold's theory, now widely accepted, stated that a river will travel along the path of least resistance. After leaving the Geological Survey in 1973, Luna became increasingly concerned about the environment. Focusing on modern agricultural practices, he was especially critical of unchecked irrigation. Luna and Estella and their brother Starker achieved an American record when all three were elected to the prestigious National Academy of Sciences.

orado Wildlife Federation in 1969 and elected to the National Academy of Sciences in 1974. Leopold was also appointed a fellow of the American Association for the Advancement of Science in 1980 and was elected to the American Academy of Arts and Sciences in 1992. She became associate editor of the scholarly journal *Quaternary Research* in 1976 and was appointed to the editorial board of *Quaternary International* in 1990. In 1998 Leopold continued to hold the position of adjunct (part-time) professor of palynology (the study of pollens and spores) and paleoecology at the University of Washington.

Further Reading

Bostick, P. E., "Paleoecology," *Magill's Survey of Science,* Volume 5, Salem Press, 1991, pp. 2037–43.

Leopold, Aldo, *A Sand County Almanac, and Sketches Here and There,* Oxford University Press, 1949.

Leopold, Estella Bergere, interview with Cynthia Washam, *Notable Twentieth-Century Scientists,* Gale, 1995, pp. 1228–29.

McGraw-Hill Encyclopedia of Science and Technology, Volume 13, McGraw-Hill, 1987, pp. 37–44.

Elsie Gregory MacGill

Born March 27, 1908
Vancouver, British Columbia, Canada
Died in 1980

Elsie Gregory MacGill was a pioneering Canadian aeronautical engineer. She became the first woman to design, build, and test an airplane. She was also the first woman to be named chief aeronautical engineer of a North American company. During World War II (1939–1945), she transformed a railway boxcar plant into an aircraft factory that produced twenty-three Hawker Hurricane fighter planes a week. A prominent consultant who was active in professional organizations after the war, MacGill is remembered as an influential figure in Canadian industrial development.

Breaks new ground

MacGill was born in Vancouver, British Columbia, Canada, on March 27, 1908. Her father was a lawyer and her mother, Helen Gregory MacGill, was British Columbia's first female juvenile court judge. MacGill chronicled her mother's life in a book titled *My Mother, the Judge* (1981). Both MacGill's mother and grandmother were active suffragettes

Elsie Gregory MacGill was the first woman to design, build, and test an airplane.

119

Aeronautical engineer Elsie Gregory MacGill was a notable figure in Canadian aircraft design and production. At a time when few women received engineering degrees, she rose to high levels of responsibility on projects for both private industry and the military. One of her greatest accomplishments was becoming the first woman to design, build, and test an airplane. MacGill reached this milestone in the 1930s with the creation of the Maple Leaf Trainer II. Her wartime service was equally impressive, as she led efforts to transform an old boxcar plant into a factory that produced high-speed Hawker Hurricane fighter planes for the British military in World War II.

(women who fought for the right to vote). As a girl, MacGill became interested in radio. This led her to study engineering at the University of Toronto where, in 1927, she became the first woman to receive a degree in electrical engineering.

MacGill then obtained a position with Austin Aircraft Company in Pontiac, Michigan. While working at the plant she also attended graduate school at the University of Michigan in Ann Arbor. Weeks before her final examinations, however, she was stricken with poliomyelitis (an acute infectious disease that causes paralysis). Because paralysis left her unable to walk, MacGill completed her exams from her hospital bed. She received the first master's degree in aeronautical engineering to be granted to a woman by the university.

MacGill then returned to Vancouver, where she earned the money to pay her hospital bills by writing articles on airplanes for popular magazines. While using a wheelchair, she designed a flying boat (a seaplane with a hull designed for floating). After MacGill had recovered enough to walk with crutches, she completed two years of doctoral work on air currents at the Massachusetts Institute of Technology (MIT). She was then employed by the Fairchild Aircraft Company in Montreal, Canada, where she applied the new technique of stress analysis to test the structure of airplane wings and fuselages (the main body of a plane). As a result of these innovations, MacGill was the first woman to read a paper before the Canadian Engineering Institute. She also became the first female member of the organization.

Builds factory

In 1937 MacGill joined the Canadian Car and Foundry Company as chief aeronautical engineer. Her first project was designing the "Maple Leaf Trainer II" plane for the Mexican Air Force. Overseeing construction and test of the aircraft before it was sent to Mexico, MacGill became the first woman in the world to design, build, and test a trainer plane.

MacGill's next endeavor was to begin Canadian production of the United Kingdom's 400-mile-per-hour Hawker Hurricane fighter planes during World War II. She directed the conversion of a boxcar factory into a Hurricane plant. Relying on 3,600 blueprints sent from England, she began retooling the plant, adapting old machines, and installing new equipment. MacGill and 120 employees worked for an entire year to convert the plant. The staff included housewives, lumbermen, trappers, and fishermen. The factory began filling its first order in January 1940, producing forty Hurricanes. This was an especially difficult task because all of the plane's 25,000 parts had to be interchangeable with their British equivalents. MacGill accompanied the Hurricane to England to test the quality of the plane's design. When a wing and a chunk of the Hawker Hurricane body were exchanged with those of a British Hurricane, the fit was perfect.

Produces Hawker Hurricanes

Production was increased after the success of the aircraft. By early 1941 a staff of 4,500 were building 23 Hurricanes per week. At the peak of production, MacGill's workers numbered 5,600—700 of whom were women. The factory also produced the first "winterized" Hurricanes, which were equipped with skis and wing and tail de-icers. MacGill later became involved in the production of the Curtiss Wright SB2C Helldiver fighter planes, which were flown from U.S. naval aircraft carriers.

Important positions and awards

In 1943 MacGill began her own aeronautics consulting firm in Toronto. After the war she served as Canadian Technical Adviser to the United Nations Civil Aviation Organization, for which she chaired the Stress Analysis Committee. MacGill was the first female member of the Association of Consulting Engineers of Canada. She was also the first female fellow of the Canadian Aeronautics and Space Institute. MacGill served as national president of the Canadian Federation of Business and Professional Women's Clubs (1962–1964) and was a member of the Engineering Institute of Canada (1965–1968). Among the awards and honors given to MacGill were the 1953 Society of Women Engineers Achievement Award, the Order of Canada (1971), and the Julian C. Smith Award from the Engineering Institute of Canada (1973). MacGill was married to business executive E. J. Soulsby.

Further Reading

Goff, Alice C., *Women Can Be Engineers,* Edwards Brothers, 1946, pp. 45–49.

Mario Molina

Born March 19, 1943
Mexico City, Mexico

Mario José Molina has made important contributions to increasing scientific understanding of the Earth's atmosphere. He gained national prominence by theorizing, with fellow atmospheric chemist F. Sherwood Rowland (1927–), that chlorofluorocarbons (CFCs) deplete the Earth's ozone layer. In 1995 Molina, Rowland, and Dutch scientist Paul Crutzen won the Nobel Prize in chemistry. During the late 1990s Molina continued his investigations into the effects of chemicals on the atmosphere as a professor at the Massachusetts Institute of Technology (MIT).

Begins career in Mexico

Molina was born in Mexico City, Mexico, on March 19, 1943, to Roberto Molina-Pasquel and Leonor Henriquez. Following his early schooling in Mexico, he graduated from the Universidad Nacional Autónoma de México in 1965 with a degree in chemical engineering. Immediately upon graduation,

Mario Molina was a corecipient of the 1995 Nobel Prize for chemistry for his work in showing how pollution destroys the ozone layer.

Portrait: Reproduced by permission of Archive Photos, Inc.

Atmospheric chemist Mario Molina made headlines in 1974 when he reported that he and F. Sherwood Rowland had discovered that chlorofluorocarbons (CFCs) could destroy the ozone layer. Scientists, politicians, and environmentalists in the United States voiced concerns about these alarming findings. In 1978 the U.S. government imposed a ban on aerosol cans, which used a CFC propellant. During the 1980s significant holes were found in the ozone layer over the South Pole. The world community then joined in a ban on the production of CFCs, which took effect in 1996. For his role in raising awareness of the dangerous effects of CFCs, Molina shared the 1995 Nobel Prize in chemistry.

Molina began attending the University of Freiburg, in West Germany. In 1967 he acquired the equivalent of a master's degree in polymerization kinetics (the study of the motion and energy involved in chemical reactions where smaller molecules join to form larger molecules). Molina then returned to Mexico to accept a position as assistant professor in the chemical engineering department at the Universidad Nacional Autónoma de México.

In 1968 Molina left Mexico to further his studies in physical chemistry at the University of California at Berkeley. He received a Ph.D. in 1972, becoming a postdoctoral associate that same year. Molina's primary area of research was the measurement of energy changes during certain chemical reactions with lasers. ("Laser" is an acronym for *l*ight *a*mplification by *s*timulated *e*mission of *r*adiation). In 1973 Molina married fellow chemist Luisa Y. Tan, with whom he later had a son, Felipe. That year Molina also left Berkeley to continue his work with physical chemist F. Sherwood Rowland at the University of California at Irvine.

Investigates CFC dangers

Molina and Rowland shared an interest in the effects of chemicals on the atmosphere. In particular, the researchers made observations of the stratosphere (the outermost section of the atmosphere that extends from about seven miles above the Earth to about thirty miles). Within the stratosphere exists the ozone layer, which protects the Earth from the Sun's harmful ultraviolet radiation. Without the ozone layer, life could not survive on Earth. Just a few years earlier, in 1970, Crutzen had shown that nitrous oxide (a chemical compound naturally pro-

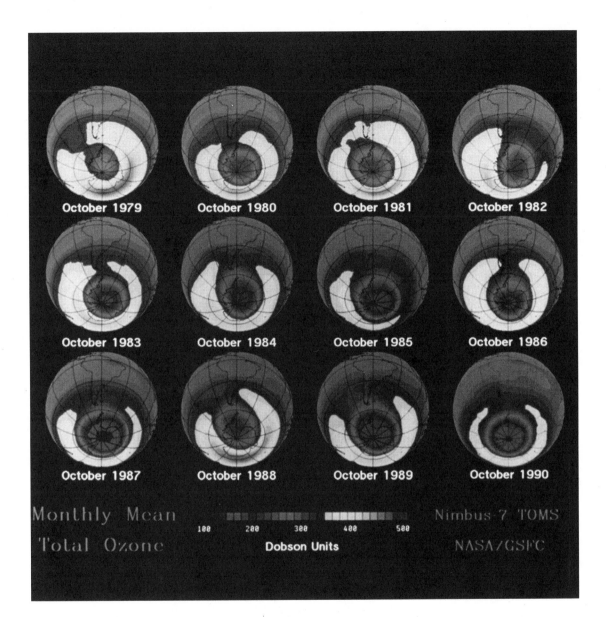

October 1979   October 1980   October 1981   October 1982

October 1983   October 1984   October 1985   October 1986

October 1987   October 1988   October 1989   October 1990

Monthly Mean Total Ozone   100   200   300   400   500   Dobson Units   Nimbus-7 TOMS   NASA/GSFC

duced by bacteria in the soil) could drift up into the stratosphere and break down ozone molecules. Molina and Rowland wondered if man-made compounds released into the atmosphere could have a similar effect.

Molina and Rowland were well aware that every year millions of tons of pollutants were pumped into the atmosphere from industrial processes. The two scientists were also

Mario Molina gained prominence by theorizing that CFCs deplete the Earth's ozone layer. Reproduced by permission of NASA.

concerned about emissions of nitrogen compounds from supersonic transport (aircraft that travel faster than the speed of sound), which the United States government was considering for development. Molina and Rowland wondered what impact these various chemical discharges could have on the air breathed by humans. As a result, they decided to conduct experiments to determine what happens to chemical pollutants that reach both the atmosphere and the stratospheric levels above.

Molina and Rowland concentrated their research on the impact of a specific group of chemicals called chlorofluorocarbons (CFCs). These chemicals are widely used in such industrial and consumer products as aerosol spray cans, pressurized containers, and refrigeration and air-conditioning coolants. The scientists found that when CFCs are subjected to massive ultraviolet radiation (invisible radiant waves or particles from the Sun), they break down into their most basic chemical parts: the elements chlorine, fluorine, and carbon. Molina and Rowland found that each chlorine atom could destroy as many as 100,000 ozone molecules before becoming inactive. They became concerned that millions of tons of CFCs were being produced each year for commercial and industrial use. They concluded that the impact of CFCs on the delicate ozone layer within the stratosphere could be life-threatening.

Report leads to CFC reduction

Molina published the results of his and Rowland's research in *Nature* magazine in 1974. The researchers' findings produced startling results. Molina was invited to testify before the U.S. House of Representatives Subcommittee on Public Health and Environment to help determine what should be done about the problem. Suddenly, CFCs were a popular topic of conversation. Manufacturers began searching for alternative propellant gases for their products. The United States government determined that the problem was so serious that in 1976 it enacted a temporary ban on the use of aerosol sprays after 1978.

In 1985 a group of British researchers found that, during certain seasons of the year, weather conditions help increase the rate of ozone destruction over the South Pole. This destruction results in an area where the ozone is much thinner than usual—what is commonly referred to as a "hole." Molina became interested in these findings and went on to investigate the cause of the problem. He suggested that ice crystals in the air over the Antarctic combine with leftover compounds from CFCs, such as chlorine nitrate and hydrochloric acid. The resulting substances are strong ozone destroyers. As ozone holes continued to appear during the 1980s and 1990s, the world community decided to follow the example of the United States. On January 1, 1996, an international agreement banned the production of CFCs.

Receives Nobel Prize

After publishing his landmark paper, Molina continued to work with Rowland. The men reported additional data on CFCs and the ozone layer in such publications as *Science* magazine. Molina was named to the National Science Foundation's Oversight Committee on Fluorocarbon Technology Assessment in 1976. He became a member of the technical staff at the Jet Propulsion Laboratory at California Polytechnic State University in 1982. In 1989 Molina left the west coast to become a chemistry professor at MIT.

Molina is the recipient of more than a dozen awards, including the American Chemical Society Esselen Award (1987), the NASA Medal for Exceptional Scientific Advancement (1989), and the United Nations Environmental Programme Global 500 Award (1989). He is also the first person not living in Mexico to be inducted into the Mexican National

Conducts Further Research

Since publishing his landmark study in *Nature* magazine in 1974, Mario Molina has continued to investigate chlorofluorocarbons, or CFCs. During the 1990s he observed the effect of CFCs on the northern hemisphere. He also examined the impact of small particles from volcanoes on the ozone layer. Another of Molina's concerns was the potential effects of supersonic transport—aircraft that travel faster than the speed of sound—on the atmosphere. Molina and his wife, Luisa Y. Tan, wrote a paper entitled "Stratospheric Ozone," which was published in the book *The Science of Global Change: The Impact of Human Activities on the Environment* (1992).

Academy of Engineers. In 1995 Molina, Rowland, and Crutzen received the scientific community's highest honor, the Nobel Prize, in the field of chemistry.

Further Readings

Levi, Barbara Goss, "Nobel Chemistry Prize Gives a Stratospheric Boost to Atmospheric Scientists," *Physics Today,* December 1995, pp. 21–22.

Lipkin, R., "Ozone Depletion Research Wins Nobel," *Science News,* October 21, 1995, p. 262.

Service, Robert F., "Uncovering Threats to the Ozone Layer Brings Rewards," *Science,* October 20, 1995, pp. 381–82.

Thomas Hunt Morgan

Born September 25, 1866
Lexington, Kentucky
Died December 4, 1945

Thomas Hunt Morgan headed a team of researchers who used *Drosophila melanogaster,* commonly known as fruit flies, to investigate how various characteristics are passed on to succeeding generations. Morgan's ideas helped to establish the study of genetics (a branch of biology that deals with the heredity and variation of organisms) as one of the most important scientific fields of the twentieth century. For his pioneering work, Morgan was awarded the Nobel Prize in Physiology, or Medicine, in 1933.

Thomas Hunt Morgan's research on fruit flies led to discoveries about the role of genes and chromosomes in heredity.

Receives education in science

Morgan was born in Lexington, Kentucky, on September 25, 1866. Members of his extended family included several famous historical figures. For instance, his uncle was the Confederate Army general who led "Morgan's Raiders" during the American Civil War (1861–1865). His great-grandfather was Francis Scott Key (1779–1893), composer of "The Star Span-

American geneticist Thomas Hunt Morgan laid the groundwork for the modern field of genetics with experiments that determined the source of inherited characteristics. Using *Drosophila melanogaster,* or fruit flies, Morgan and his research team discovered how genetic information carried on chromosomes is responsible for the traits of an organism. This finding disproved the popular theory that environmental factors are involved in determining many traits. Morgan's discoveries helped form the basis for the mapping of genes, which had a significant impact on medicine and other scientific fields.

gled Banner." During his childhood, Morgan spent two summers working with the U.S. Geological Survey in the Kentucky mountains. In 1886 he received a bachelor's degree in zoology (the study of animal life) from the State College of Kentucky (which later became the University of Kentucky). That same year he entered Johns Hopkins University in Baltimore, Maryland, where he studied embryology (a branch of biology dealing with embryos, or animals in the early stages of development).

At Johns Hopkins, Morgan was taught comparative anatomy (comparing the structures of one organism to those of another) and embryology as a method for determining the nature of life. He studied the embryology of sea spiders in an attempt to classify these organisms as either arachnids (insects such as spiders) or crustaceans (aquatic creatures such as crayfish). After receiving a Ph.D. from Johns Hopkins in 1890, Morgan sought less rigid methods of experimentation. The following year he went to Bryn Mawr College in Pennsylvania. At Bryn Mawr he was influenced by mechanistic views, which state that living things are governed by certain laws and principles. In 1904 Morgan married Lilian Vaughan Sampson, a student of cell biology at Bryn Mawr, who later made important contributions to his research. During that year Morgan also took a position as head of experimental zoology at Columbia University in New York, New York.

Heredity or environment?

While Morgan was conducting his studies in the United States, a controversy was brewing in Europe over the factors governing the development of the embryo. Some scientists believed development is dictated by heredity (the genetic

A fruit fly. Thomas Hunt Morgan's research team used fruit flies in its studies to discover how genetic information carried on chromosomes is responsible for the traits of an organism. Reproduced by permission of UPI/Corbis-Bettmann.

information inherited an organism inherits from its parents). Conversely, others felt that environmental factors outside the embryo are responsible for its journey from a fertilized egg to a recognizable member of its species.

Morgan then studied the eggs of sea urchins (marine animals that have a thin brittle shell covered with movable spines). His observations led him to believe that the environment may indeed help shape an embryo's development, but that inheritance is the more influential factor. These findings made Morgan even more curious about the hereditary information carried by each cell. He was especially interested in the question of which chemical and physical processes control inheritance of that information.

From 1903 to 1910 Morgan concentrated on the determination of sex in living things, a much-debated scientific topic at the time. Some scientists contended that the sex of an organism is determined by environmental factors, such as weather temperature or food supply. Others claimed it is a matter of inheritance, citing the work of Austrian scientist Gregor Mendel (see entry in volume two). Mendel's experiments on the inheritance of pea plants had just been rediscovered. Mendel had postulated that all of an organism's traits were caused by inherited factors, which he was unable to identify. Some scientists speculated that these factors, which could be found within chromosomes (bodies of viruses in a cell), contain all inherited characteristics. They named the factors "genes."

Morgan agreed that chromosomes probably did have something to do with inheritance. He was skeptical of Mendel's laws of inheritance, however, thinking that they were too simplistic to explain sex determination. During the early days of his research, Morgan did not believe that the sex of an organism was determined at the moment of fertilization (the union of egg and sperm). Instead he suspected that sex resulted from a developmental process guided by natural law. Finally, observing sex inheritance in some insects, Morgan came to realize that the presence of chromosomes must have something to do with inheriting sex. Around 1910 his colleagues at Bryn Mawr and Columbia gathered evidence to show that a large chromosome, which they called the "X" chromosome, had the most influence on sex inheritance.

Conducts fruit fly research

In the early 1900s Morgan began breeding fruit flies for laboratory experiments. He originally wanted to use the insects to test certain theories of mutation in animals by exposing them to radium (a radioactive metallic element that emits alpha particles and gamma rays). Morgan's efforts were not entirely successful. Then in 1910 he discovered a natural variation in a male fruit fly—it had white eyes instead of red eyes. After Morgan mated the white-eyed males with red-eyed females, he found that all the offspring had red eyes. The mating of those red-eyed flies, however, produced a generation in which there were some white-eyed offspring, all of which were male.

Although Morgan had earlier been skeptical of such attributes as eye color being inherited so precisely, he now found himself explaining this phenomenon in terms of Mendel's factors, or genes. He hypothesized that the genes for eye color were carried on, and therefore linked to, the X chromosome. This type of gene became known as a sex-limited or sex-linked gene. Morgan further hypothesized that a fly would possess white eyes only if all of its X chromosomes possessed the white-eye gene. Since male flies have only one X chromosome, the gene becomes recessive (less likely to be expressed). They were more likely to display this recessive trait than females, which have two X chromosomes carrying red genes that become dominant (most often expressed). With this experiment, Morgan showed that hereditary characteristics are associated with specific chromosomes.

Team sets up "fly room"

After achieving this breakthrough, Morgan began a more intensive fruit-fly breeding project with the help of several other scientists. Among them were undergraduate students A. H. Sturtevant (1891–1970) and Calvin B. Bridges (1889–1938) and graduate student Hermann Joseph Muller (1890–1967). For their research project, Morgan's team maintained a winter lab at Columbia University and a summer lab at the Marine Biological Laboratory in Woods Hole, Massachusetts. Together the two labs were known as the "fly room." The fly room became a proving ground for future geneticists, especially Muller, who went on to win the Nobel Prize in 1946.

The project soon produced successful results, as new mutations appeared and were carefully tracked. The flies

Criticizes Natural Selection

In 1903 Geneticist Thomas Hunt Morgan published *Evolution and Adaptation,* an attack on the theory of natural selection, which was formulated by English naturalist Charles Darwin. Noting that Darwin's supporters relied too heavily on natural selection, Morgan asserted that no single theory could explain the origins of all living organisms. Morgan preferred ideas introduced by Dutch botanist Hugo de Vries (1848–1935), who proposed that mutations can occur in individuals within a population. These individual changes can then cause variations necessary for evolutionary development. In 1916 Morgan modified his criticism of natural selection in *A Critique of the Theory of Evolution.* Rather than discounting the theory, Morgan used his new understanding of chromosome mutation to offer a genetic explanation for Darwin's discoveries.

proved to be ideal test subjects, having a breeding cycle of just three weeks and possessing only four chromosomes that carried all the genes for their traits. Because the actual genes could not be seen, the team concluded that a particular part of each chromosome carried a certain trait. This assumption was based on a phenomenon called "crossing over," which had been discovered by Belgian scientist F. A. Janssens in 1909.

Use mapping technique

Janssens had noticed that during the process of chromosome duplication, part of one chromosome occasionally broke off and reattached to a similar place on another. He also found that the farther apart two genes were on a single chromosome, the more likely a break could occur between them. Janssens concluded that a high frequency of crossing over between any two traits would indicate a long distance between the genes. In contrast, a low frequency of crossing over between two traits would indicate that the genes are close together. Morgan's team member Sturtevant devised a method of using this information to "map" each chromosome. The team then applied this mapping technique to show how various genes for a particular trait might be arranged along each chromosome. The group published the results of their work in *The Mechanism of Mendelian Heredity* (1915), which gave the new experimental science of genetics a place in the world of biology.

Receives awards and honors

In the 1920s Morgan moved on from fruit flies to address larger issues of genetics. In 1927 he left Columbia for the California Institute of Technology (Cal Tech) in Pasadena, California, where he established a biology department. Morgan's Cal Tech team helped pioneer the next wave of genetics research, exploring the molecules (small particles containing one or more atoms) of genes. In 1933 Morgan won the Nobel Prize for Physiology, or Medicine, for his advances in the field of genetics. During his career Morgan served as the president of both the Association for the Advancement of Science and the National Academy of Sciences. In 1939 he was awarded the Copley Medal of the Royal Society in England. Morgan continued doing administrative work at Cal Tech until his death in 1945.

Further Reading

Biographical Memoirs: National Academy of Sciences, Volume 33, 1959, pp. 283–325.

Dictionary of Scientific Biography, Scribner's, 1985, pp. 515–26.

Margaret Morse Nice

Born December 6, 1883
Amherst, Massachusetts

Died June 26, 1974
Chicago, Illinois

Margaret Morse Nice was a pioneering ornithologist and ethologist who studied and wrote about birds.

Margaret Morse Nice became one of America's leading ornithologists by stressing the importance of studying the behavior of individual birds to better understand the nature of each species as a whole. Despite the fact that she never held a university position or received research funding, her detailed observations had a lasting impact on the fields of ornithology (the study of birds) and ethology (the study of animal behavior). Nice was also a traditional homemaker, and she made most of her contributions by investigating birds in her own backyard.

Observes birds as a child

Nice was born on December 6, 1883, in Amherst, Massachusetts, to Anson and Margaret (Ely) Morse. Her father was an Amherst College history professor as well as a gardener with a deep love of the wilderness. Nice's mother had studied botany (the science of plant life) at Mount Holyoke College in

Massachusetts. She helped inspire her daughter's curiosity about nature by teaching her the name of wildflowers as they walked in the woods. Nice became interested in ornithology at an early age. In fact, she was recording observations of birds by the time she was twelve.

After attending a private elementary school and the public high school in Amherst, Nice enrolled at Mount Holyoke College in 1901. At first she studied languages, then later switched to the natural sciences. Upon graduating from Mount Holyoke in 1906, Nice received a fellowship to study biology for two years at Clark University in Worcester, Massachusetts. During this time she conducted research on bobwhites and published her first paper, "The Food of the Bob-white," in the *Journal of Economic Entomology* (1910). In 1909 she married Leonard Blaine Nice and the couple moved to Cambridge, Massachusetts, where Leonard entered Harvard Medical School. In 1913 they went to Norman, Oklahoma, where Leonard had been appointed head of the physiology department at the University of Oklahoma.

Compiles book on Oklahoma birds

Over the next several years Nice gave birth to five daughters and devoted her time to being a mother. Frustrated at not being able to continue her studies in ornithology, she began observing how her daughters acquired language. With this work she earned a master's degree in psychology from Clark University in 1915. She eventually published eighteen articles on child psychology.

Nice was encouraged to return to the study of birds by Althea Sherman, a friend and amateur ornithologist. In 1920

Nice published the first of thirty-five articles about Oklahoma bird life. Four years later she and her husband coauthored *The Birds of Oklahoma*. By this time Nice's studies had become a family affair. For instance, her husband would assist with bird counts, and her daughters would climb trees to check bird nests for eggs. During these early years, Nice's work often involved simply cataloguing the number of bird species (classes) in an area and noting the distribution of bird populations. She had a practice, however, of keeping injured or abandoned wild birds as pets in her house. By closely watching their activities, Nice began to develop an interest in animal behavior.

Researches territorial behavior

In 1927 Leonard Nice took a teaching position in Columbus, Ohio, and the family moved to a house on the bank of the Olentangy River. Since the site attracted a number of nesting and migratory birds (species that move from one place to another) such as song sparrows, Nice decided to study the territorial behavior of birds. She placed colored bands on individual birds, then watched them over a period of several years. Nice's data included information on mating and parenting behaviors and singing habits. Her studies resulted in several publications, the most notable being the two-part *Studies in the Life History of the Song Sparrow* (1937 and 1943). As a result of this ground-breaking research, she became one of the world's leading ornithologists. In an introduction to Nice's autobiography, *Research Is a Passion with Me* (1979), Austrian ethologist Konrad Lorenz wrote that her work on the song sparrow was "the first long-term investigation of the individual life of any free-living wild animal." *Notable American Women* quoted German evolutionary biologist Ernst Mayr (1904– ; see entry in volume five) as saying that Nice had "almost singlehandedly, initiated a new era in American ornithology."

Two song sparrows. Margaret Morse Nice became one of America's leading ornithologists by stressing the importance of studying the behavior of individual birds, including sparrows and bobwhites. Reproduced by permission of Corbis-Bettmann.

Turns attention to conservation

In 1936 Nice and her family moved to Chicago, Illinois, where her husband had accepted an appointment at the University of Chicago Medical School. Although she was no longer able to conduct extensive field observations, Nice continued to study and write. With her knowledge of languages, including German and Dutch, she exposed Americans to European ornithology in reviews and translations of articles. Nice also wrote *The Watcher at the Nest,* (1939), a book about bird watching intended for a general audience. Selling only a few copies upon publication, it later became a classic among bird watchers. During this period Nice was an active conservationist, advocating the preservation of wildlife and calling for restricted use of pesticides (chemicals used to destroy insects).

Honored for contributions

As head of the Wilson Ornithological Society in 1938 and 1939, Nice became the first woman president of a major American ornithological society. She was also associate editor of the journal *Bird-Banding* (1935–1942 and 1946–1974). She was awarded the Brewster Medal of the American Ornithologists' Union in 1942 and received an honorary doctorate from Mount Holyoke College in 1955. In 1969 the Wilson Ornithological Society inaugurated a grant in Nice's name that would be given to self-trained amateur researchers. Nice died in Chicago at the age of ninety.

Further Reading

Bailey, Martha J., *American Women in Science: A Biographical Dictionary,* ABC-Clio, 1994, pp. 268–69.

Konrad Lorenz, Ethologist

Nobel Prize-winning Austrian scientist Konrad Lorenz was a pioneer in the field of ethology. Throughout his career he published several important books, including *King Solomon's Ring* (1952), an account of animal behavior. Despite his success, Lorenz received criticism for *On Aggression* (1966), in which he contended that the fighting instinct is necessary for the survival of both humans and animals. His best-known work is *The Year of the Greylag Goose* (1978), which introduced the concept of imprinting (an early learning process in which behavior patterns are established through association with role models).

Bonta, Marcia Byers, *Women in the Field: America's Pioneering Women Naturalists,* Texas A & M University Press, 1991, pp. 222–31.

Conway, Jill K., editor, *Written by Herself,* Vintage Books, 1991.

Nice, Margaret Morse, with Leonard Blaine Nice, *The Birds of Oklahoma,* University of Oklahoma, 1924; revised edition, 1931.

Nice, Margaret Morse, *Research Is a Passion with Me,* Consolidated Amethyst, 1979.

Nice, Margaret Morse, *Studies in the Life History of the Song Sparrow,* two volumes, [New York], 1937 and 1943.

Nice, Margaret Morse, *The Watcher at the Nest,* Macmillan, 1939.

Sicherman, Barbara, and Carol Hurd Green, eds. *Notable American Women: The Modern Period,* Belknap, 1980, pp. 506–7.

Trautman, Milton B., "In Memoriam: Margaret Morse Nice," *The Auk,* July 1977.

Roger Penrose

Born August 8, 1931
Colchester, England

Roger Penrose has explored a range of topics in mathematical theory and physics. Among his interests are relativity theory, quantum mechanics, astrophysics, cosmology, possible and impossible geometric shapes, and how the human brain works. A self described "dabbler," Penrose has produced several influential theories and discoveries. With English theoretical physicist and professor Stephen Hawking (see entry in volume two), he extended scientific understanding of black holes and the big bang theory of the origin of the universe. His work with geometric puzzles has shed light on the nature of quasi-crystals, which are made from complex, irregular patterns of atoms. Having turned to the study of the workings of human consciousness, Penrose has suggested that this phenomenon may be understood only through a new, and as yet undiscovered, realm of physics.

Studies mathematics and physics

Penrose was born August 8, 1931, in Colchester, England, into an educated and accomplished family. His father, Lionel S.

Roger Penrose is a leading mathematician and physicist who helped to prove the existence of black holes.

Mathematician and physicist Roger Penrose has made contributions to a variety of scientific fields. With English theoretical physicist Stephen Hawking, he developed proofs for the existence of black holes. Penrose and Hawking also showed that forces at the heart of black holes were involved in the "big bang" that is believed to have been the origin of the universe. Pursuing his interest in geometrical patterns known as tilings, Penrose developed an irregular tiling that helped scientists to understand the nature of crystals with similar configurations. Known as "quasi-crystals," these structures may allow scientists to develop new, super-strong synthetic materials for use in research and industry. Penrose has also investigated how physics can help explain the workings of human consciousness.

Penrose, was a geneticist, and his mother, Margaret Newman, was a physician. As a young boy, Penrose shared his father's interest in nature and geometrical puzzles. In school he showed a talent for mathematics by devising geometry problems that challenged his teachers. Penrose studied mathematics at University College, London, receiving a bachelor of science degree in 1952. Five years later he earned a Ph.D. from Cambridge University, where he wrote his dissertation on algebraic geometry.

While he was still a student, Penrose rediscovered and developed the generalized inverse matrix (a method of solving equations that involves rectangular arrangements of numbers), which was introduced by American mathematician Eliakim Hastings Moore (1862–1932). At St. John's College, Cambridge, Penrose heard lectures by English physicist Paul Dirac (1902–1984) on quantum mechanics (the behavior of subatomic particles) and by Austrian-British mathematician Hermann Bondi (1919–) on the theory of relativity (pertaining to the relationship between space, time, and matter). These experiences sparked Penrose's interest in relating quantum mechanics and space-time structure. (Space-time structure is a view of the universe from the perspective of four dimensions, which includes the three dimensions people observe in everyday life, plus the fourth dimension of time.)

Develops mathematics of black holes

In 1965 Penrose expanded on the theory of general relativity developed by German-born American physicist Albert Einstein (see entry in volume one). Penrose showed that in

space there must be infinitely dense and hot points called singularities (points within a black hole where gravitational pull is infinite). According to Penrose, the laws of classical physics (the science of the motion of bodies larger than the atomic level) do not apply to singularities because the gravitational field becomes infinite, or other abnormal behavior occurs. Penrose's theorem proved that if a star of sufficient mass collapses, a singularity will result. His work convinced physicists of the existence of black holes, inspiring the search for these bizarre structures.

A year later Hawking, who was working at Cambridge University in England, applied Penrose's theorem to cosmology (the study of the origin and structure of the universe). Hawking proved that the universe started in a singularity. In 1970 Penrose and Hawking collaborated to prove a singularity theorem that was much more powerful than their earlier efforts. Previous research had indicated that the universe did

A possible black hole as seen from a nearby asteroid. Roger Penrose's research convinced physicists of the existence of black holes and inspired the search for these bizarre structures. Reproduced by permission of David Hardy. Science Photo Library, National Audubon Collection/Photo Researchers, Inc.

not begin with a big bang singularity. Penrose and Hawking's theorem challenged this view, asserting that in any universe with certain fundamental properties, a big bang singularity must occur. Penrose further contributed to Hawking's work on black holes by using mathematical theories to show that the surface area of a black hole must increase as mass is added.

In order to explain black holes, Penrose was aided by his invention of the "twistor," a mathematical tool for describing physical objects and space. The twistor incorporates energy, momentum, and spin, which are the three properties possessed by all objects moving through space and time. A twistor has either six or eight dimensions, each of which involves either movement or change in size.

Invents tribar

Penrose's primary area of research is tiling (the complete covering of a flat surface with a regular pattern of tiles). His theories were influenced by other mathematicians, including seventeenth-century German mathematician and astronomer Johannes Kepler (see entry in volume four). He was also inspired by the drawings of Dutch artist M. C. Escher (1898–1970). While doing graduate studies in 1954, Penrose saw Escher's work at a mathematics conference in Amsterdam, Holland. The artist had incorporated geometry and perspective to produce drawings of "impossible" objects. Penrose was fascinated with these illustrations of objects that go against the rules of three-dimensional reality. He proceeded to draw his own similar construct, a "tribar" of three beams, which he sent to Escher. The artist later used the tribar figure as the basis for a continuous flow of water in his lithograph (an artwork, also called a print) *Waterfall*.

Finds tiling gaps

The simplest tiling pattern utilizes identical tiles of equilateral (equal on all sides) shapes such as squares (shapes with four equal sides), triangles (shapes with three equal sides), or hexagons (shapes with six equal sides). However, regular pentagons (shapes with five equal sides) will not tile a surface without leaving gaps. Penrose found that a floor or any other plane (flat surface) can be covered with pentagons and two other shapes, which are stars and hat-shaped pieces. The resulting pattern has regularities but does not repeat itself exactly. Some tiling patterns repeat themselves in a certain way. Patterns can be matched by placing a sheet of paper over the design, and then moving the paper sideways without rotating it. Such designs are called "periodic."

Develops nonperiodic tilings

Penrose's pattern was nonperiodic. With some tile designs, such as hexagons, the neighboring tiles will indicate where to put the next one. Such patterns are called "local." Penrose's pattern appeared to be nonlocal. Penrose worked with pieces of various shapes, trying to find the smallest number of shapes that would force a nonperiodic tiling. He discovered several combinations, and finally, in 1974, lowered the number of shapes to two. One of his most interesting designs used two shapes derived from a rhombus (a parallelogram made up of four sides of equal length). In this design one piece looked like a kite and the other resembled a dart. Following rules about which edges could be fitted together, the two shapes forced a non-periodic tiling.

Inspires quasi-crystal research

In the 1980s crystallographers (scientists who study the structure of crystals) became interested in Penrose's findings. For a century, scientists had thought that the atoms in crystals were arranged periodically and that crystals with five-fold symmetry were impossible. (Five-fold symmetry describes an object that has an identical structure on both sides of five different dividing lines, or axis.) But in studying an alloy (combination of substances) of aluminum and manganese, Dan Schechtman at the National Bureau of Standards saw what appeared to be nonperiodic crystals with five-fold symmetry. The complicated sequences in the pattern were only partially, or "quasi," periodic. Halfway between crystals and glass-like structures, this new form of matter was called a quasi-crystal. The quasi-crystal caused considerable excitement among chemists, physicists, and crystallographers. The similarity between the quasi-crystal and the Penrose patterns was recognized by University of Pennsylvania physicist Paul Steinhardt and crystallographer Alan MacKay of London.

In 1988 Steinhardt and George Onoda, an IBM ceramics expert, devised rules for building a Penrose tiling. These results provided possible clues to the growth of three-dimensional quasi-crystals. Researchers proceeded to study the properties of the new alloys. Because of the intricate structure of the crystals, it was thought that the alloys might turn out to be harder than crystals and usable as substitutes for industrial diamonds or as materials in electronic devices.

Discounts artificial intelligence

In 1989 Penrose published *The Emperor's New Mind: Concerning Computers, Minds, and the Laws of Physics,* which was on the *New York Times* best-seller list for nine weeks. In the book Penrose disagrees with a view held by some researchers in the field of artificial intelligence, that computers are capable of mimicking the function of human brains. A computer program, Penrose argues, uses an algorithm (a step-by-step mechanical procedure) for working toward an answer. Because certain kinds of human thinking are nonalgorithmic (not able to be expressed in a mathematical formula) Penrose suggests that the physical activities of the human brain must be making use of nonalgorithmic processes.

Penrose notes that current theories of physics cannot handle the nonalgorithmic realities of the human mind. He suspects that a greater understanding of the functioning of the human brain may depend on a fundamentally new understanding of physics. Penrose continued his investigation of this topic in *Shadows of the Mind: A Search for the Missing Science of Consciousness* (1994) and *The Large, the Small, and the Human Mind* (1997), a collaboration with other scientists.

Receives awards and honors

Throughout his career, Penrose taught and conducted research at major universities in England and the United States. He was a research fellow at St. John's College, Cambridge (1957–1960). He was also a North Atlantic Treaty Organization (NATO) research fellow at Princeton, Syracuse, and Cornell universities (1959–1961). During the 1960s he had visiting appointments at the University of Chicago, the University of California at Berkeley, and Bedford College in London. In 1973 Penrose was named the Rouse Ball professor at Oxford University in England. In the 1980s he was the Edgar Odell Lovett Professor of Mathematics at Rice University in Houston, Texas. His early honors included the Adams Prize from Cambridge University (1966) and prizes from the American Physical Society and the American Institute of Physics (both 1971). Penrose was elected to the Royal Society in 1972. For their study of black holes, Penrose and Hawking shared the Royal Astronomical Society's Eddington Medal in 1975 and were also awarded the Wolf Foundation Prize in Physics in 1988.

Further Reading

Gardner, Martin, *Penrose Tiles to Trapdoor Ciphers,* W. H. Freeman and Co., 1989.

Horgan, John, "The Artist, the Physicist and the Waterfall," *Scientific American,* February 1993, p. 30.

Horgan, John, "Quantum Consciousness: Polymath Roger Penrose Takes on the Ultimate Mystery," *Scientific American,* November 1989, pp. 31–33.

"Interview: Roger Penrose," *Omni,* June 1986, pp. 67–68, 70, 73, 106–7.

Landauer, Rolf, "Is the Mind More Than an Analytic Engine?," *Physics Today,* June 1990, pp. 73–75.

"Many-sided Penrose," *The Economist,* September 17, 1988, p. 100.

McGraw-Hill Modern Scientists and Engineers, Volume 2, McGraw-Hill, 1980, pp. 407-8.

Penrose, Roger, *The Emperor's New Mind: Concerning Computers, Minds, and the Laws of Physics,* Oxford University Press, 1989.

Siegel, Matthew, "Wolf Foundation Honors Hawking and Penrose for Work on Relativity," *Physics Today,* January 1989, pp. 97–98.

von Baeyer, Hans C., "Impossible Crystals," *Discover,* February 1990, pp. 69–78.

Gifford Pinchot

Born August 11, 1865
Simsbury, Connecticut
Died October 4, 1946
New York, New York

ifford Pinchot was a pioneer of the forestry movement and the first American to receive formal training in forestry. Beginning with his work in the Biltmore Forest of North Carolina, he established the practice of scientifically-based forest management. Pinchot served under three presidents, William McKinley (1843–1901), Theodore Roosevelt (1858–1919), and William Howard Taft (1857–1930). As chief of the Forest Service, he was a major force in the political world and a sometimes controversial figure. Pinchot often drew criticism from many conservationists of his day for his belief that forests should be used, not simply preserved.

Gifford Pinchot established the scientific study and practice of forestry in the United States.

Designs own forestry curriculum

Born August 11, 1865, in Simsbury, Connecticut, Pinchot was the first of four children of James Wallace Pinchot, a wealthy New York merchant, and Mary Jane (Eno) Pinchot. The Pinchot children were raised in an atmosphere rich in

Portrait: Reproduced by permission of Corbis-Bettmann.

Forester and politician Gifford Pinchot was instrumental in developing the management structure of national forests in the United States. The first American to pursue the scientific study of forestry, Pinchot brought back ideas from Europe and Asia. In his role as head of the National Forest Service, he applied these innovations to American forests. Pinchot believed that the best way to support a forest is to use its resources to help pay for its maintenance, a policy that is still in effect. Among Pinchot's other contributions to conservation was the Civilian Conservation Corps, a Depression-era work force that undertook numerous projects, including planting trees in deforested areas.

French culture, and they were exposed to important personalities in the arts and politics. Pinchot attended private schools in New York and Paris as well as the Phillips Exeter Academy at Andover, Massachusetts.

In 1885 Pinchot entered Yale University in New Haven, Connecticut. Following the advice of his father, he decided to become a professional forester. Like other American universities at the time, Yale did not offer courses in forestry. Pinchot therefore designed his own curriculum by taking courses in botany (the study of plant life), meteorology (the study of the atmosphere, particularly the weather), and other sciences. After receiving a bachelor of science degree in 1889, he traveled to London, England, to study the forestry program the British government had implemented in India. He also attended the National Forestry School in Nancy, France, where he studied silviculture (tree-growing) and forest economics. His analysis of forest management in European countries convinced him that the right approach would be to treat forests as a public resource. When Pinchot returned home in 1890, he was determined to introduce the concept of public forestry in the United States.

Begins forestry career

In 1892 Pinchot was hired to manage the neglected Biltmore Forest, located on the North Carolina estate of railroad magnate George Vanderbilt (1862–1914). In his new post Pinchot had the opportunity to apply the principles of scientific forestry that he had observed in Europe. Within a year he was able to show a profit at Biltmore. In 1894 Pinchot left North Carolina to set up his own consulting business in New York

City. Traveling throughout the United States, he visited the nation's forest reserves. As a supporter of controlled commercial use of public and private forests, Pinchot favored selective harvesting and other measures to promote the well-being and regrowth of forests.

Takes government post

In 1896 Pinchot was appointed to the newly created National Forest Commission of the National Academy of Sciences. A year later the commission's study of national forest reserves in the western United States resulted in the passage of the Forest Management Act. This was the legal framework that guided the commercial use of national forest reserves. In 1897 Pinchot was offered a post in the United States Division of Forestry. The following year he was chosen to succeed Dr. Bernhard E. Fernow (1851–1923) as chief of the small agency, which was part of the U.S. Department of Agriculture.

After taking his new post Pinchot began a campaign for transferring the control of United States forest reserves from the Interior Department to the Department of Agriculture. He accomplished his goal in 1905 and the division was renamed the Forest Service. Two years later the reserves became known as national forests. The success of Pinchot's mission largely depended on the support of President Roosevelt, with whom Pinchot developed a close working relationship and friendship. Pinchot's administration of the nation's forests resulted in an increase from 51 million acres in 1901 to 175 million by 1910.

Popularizes conservation

Joining Roosevelt in making conservation a popular topic in America, Pinchot helped formulate the conservation policies of the president's administration. He worked to obtain a standard system of classification of the nation's natural resources by the U.S. Geographical Survey. In 1908, while serving on the Inland Waterways Commission, he was instrumental in starting regional development of America's river

Environmentalist Challenges Pinchot

Environmentalist Aldo Leopold (see entry in volume five) laid the groundwork for many U.S. conservation laws. In 1908 he graduated from Yale University in New Haven, Connecticut. At the time, Yale embraced the conservation philosophy of Gifford Pinchot, who believed in the economic value of nature. Following his Yale colleagues, Leopold initially accepted Pinchot's ideas. After joining the U.S. Forest Service in 1909, however, Leopold began to revise his views. Leopold's conservation campaign led to the creation of America's first federal reserve in New Mexico in 1924. He was also instrumental in formulating the Environmental Policy Act (1969) and the Endangered Species Act (1973). Leopold was the father of Luna and Estella Bergere Leopold (see entry), who also made important contributions to science and conservation. (Portrait: Reproduced by permission of AP/Wide World Photos.)

systems. That same year Pinchot also organized the White House Conference on the Conservation of Natural Resources. He served as chair of the resulting National Conservation Commission, which prepared an inventory of the country's natural resources.

Pinchot's fortunes began to decline, however, when Taft succeeded Roosevelt as president. Losing his favored position, Pinchot faced hostility from Richard A. Ballinger (1858–1922), the Secretary of the Interior. Taft himself opposed many of Pinchot's conservation policies and attempted to undermine the smooth functioning of the Forest Service. In the power struggle that followed, Pinchot was dismissed from government service for publicly criticizing the president.

Begins political career

Prompted by a commitment to public service, Pinchot increasingly turned his attention to politics. He campaigned against the reelection of Taft, helped found the National Progressive Republican League in 1911, and worked within the new Progressive Party for the renomination of Roosevelt for president in 1912. On August 14, 1914, Pinchot married Cornelia Elizabeth Bryce, with whom he later had a son, Gifford Bryce. A suffragist (supporter of women's right to vote), Cornelia was an adviser to Pinchot and helped to guide his career.

Pinchot was known for his strong views. In 1914 he made an unsuccessful run for the U.S. Senate against Pennsylvania Senator Boies Penrose (1860–1921). Pinchot favored extreme positions such as government ownership of railroads,

Civilian Conservation Corps, or CCC, workers in the Lassen Volcanic National Forest, 1933. A memo written by Gifford Pinchot to President Franklin D. Roosevelt resulted in the creation of the CCC, which recruited young men for reforestation projects during the Great Depression. Reproduced by permission of Capt. Daniel Sheehan. USDA-Forest Service/ Corbis-Bettmann.

public utilities, and industries such as coal, copper, and lumber. After making another unsuccessful Senate attempt in 1920, he became forestry commissioner of Pennsylvania. Still determined to secure a political office, Pinchot was finally elected governor of Pennsylvania in 1922.

The high point of Pinchot's first term was the reform of government operations and state finances. Although he was reelected in 1930, conflicts over public utilities prevented him from making any major accomplishments. Pinchot nevertheless managed to create jobs during the Great Depression (an era of widespread economic hardship, 1929–1939). His later campaigns for various other political offices were unsuccessful.

Remains active conservationist

Through the years Pinchot continued his interest in conservation. He played a key role in the passage of laws such as the Weeks Act (1911) and the Water Power Act (1920). Pinchot became a nonresident lecturer and professor at the Yale School of Forestry, which had been established in 1900 by a grant from his family. He also founded and served as president of the Society of American Foresters. A memorandum Pinchot drafted for President Franklin D. Roosevelt (1882–1945) resulted in the creation of the Civilian Conservation Corps (CCC), which recruited young men for reforestation projects. Pinchot's autobiography, *Breaking New Ground* (1947)— which was published a year after his death—is considered an important conservation document.

Further Reading

Faber, Doris, and Harold Faber, *Great Lives ... Nature and the Environment*, Charles Scribner's Sons, 1991.

Journal of Forestry (Gifford Pinchot Commemorative Issue), August 1965.

McGeary, M. Nelson, *Gifford Pinchot: Forester-Politician*, Princeton University Press, 1960.

Pinchot, Gifford, *Breaking New Ground*, Harcourt, 1947.

Pinkett, Harold T., *Gifford Pinchot: Private and Public Forester,* University of Illinois Press, 1970.

Squire, C. B., *Heroes of Conservation,* Fleet Press, 1974.

Watkins, T. H., "Father of the Forests," *American Heritage,* February/March 1991, pp. 86–98.

Ptolemy

Born c. A.D. 100
Egypt
Died c. A.D. 170
Egypt

Ptolemy was responsible for popularizing the geocentric theory of the universe— the idea that all heavenly bodies rotate around the Earth.

The second-century mathematician and astronomer Ptolemy served as a bridge from the ancient Greeks to the scholars and scientists of the Middle Ages (400–1400) and the Renaissance (1400–1600). Ptolemy provided clear, logical explanations of the scientific thinking of Greek astronomers such as Hipparchus (146 B.C.–127 B.C.). His writings were therefore accepted as scientific truth for hundreds of years. One of Ptolemy's most influential ideas was the geocentric (Earth-centered) theory of the universe. This concept was not questioned until Polish astronomer Nicholas Copernicus (see entry in volume four) presented a heliocentric (Sun-centered) theory of the universe in the 1500s.

Conducts studies in Alexandria

Very little is known about Ptolemy's life. He was probably born around A.D. 100 in Egypt. Some historians have suggested that his birthplace was Ptolemais Hermii, a city in Upper Egypt populated by Greeks (which would explain the source of his name). Historians know that he lived and worked in Alexandria, Egypt, because he mentions the city in his books as the site of his astronomical observations. Since Alexandria had a Greek population, Ptolemy probably had Greek ancestors. He is also known by the Latin name Claudius Ptolemaeus, suggesting that someone in his family had been awarded Roman citizenship, a status that was passed on to later generations.

Develops modern trigonometry

Alexandria was once the center of learning in the ancient world. By Ptolemy's time, however, most of the city's glory had been lost. In spite of this loss, scientists were still able to use its fine libraries. Ptolemy probably became familiar with the work of earlier Greek thinkers at Alexandria. Ptolemy's primary contribution to scientific history was the compilation, explanation, and improvement upon the work of the ancient Greeks. The scientist most frequently quoted by Ptolemy was Hipparchus, often considered the father of astronomy (the study of objects and matter outside the Earth's atmosphere). Ptolemy compiled a series of books covering various areas of mathematical science, including astronomy, geography, optics, and music. Building on Hipparchus's invention of spherical trigonometry (the study of spheres) and plane trigonometry (the study of triangles), Ptolemy perfected this area of mathematics. His theorems have remained intact as the basis of modern trigonometry.

IMPACT

The second-century Egyptian astronomer and mathematician Ptolemy had a powerful impact on scientific thinking for over one thousand years. His Ptolemaic system, a concept based on the writings of Greek astronomer Hipparchus, stated that the universe was Earth-centered. Ptolemy's method of calculating planetary positions seemed to provide accurate predictions. In fact, Ptolemy's technique was not seriously questioned until Polish astronomer Nicholas Copernicus presented his Sun-centered theory of the planetary system in the 1500s. The Ptolemaic system was finally abandoned in the 1600s, after German astronomer Johannes Kepler found a more accurate explanation for the movement of the planets. Kepler discovered that planets travel in elliptical, instead of circular, orbits around the Sun.

Almagest presents Ptolemaic system

Ptolemy had perhaps his most significant impact on astronomy. In *Mega mathematike syntaxis* ("Great mathematical compilation"), which was probably the earliest of his written works, he compiled a thirteen-volume description of the universe. Some scholars called the book *Megiste* ("Greatest"). When Arab scientists translated the work, they used the Arabic "al" ("the") in front of the title, and so the book came to be known as *Almagest.* Translated into Latin in 1175, the work soon became the ultimate astronomical authority in Europe.

The *Almagest* expanded on the work of Hipparchus, who made a catalogue of stars and grouped them into forty-eight constellations. Ptolemy gave the constellations names that are still used today. He also incorporated Hipparchus's work on trigonometry, as well as his fairly accurate estimate of the distance between the Earth and the Moon. (Ptolemy used an incorrect estimate of the Earth's distance from the Sun, however, that had been calculated by Greek astronomer Aristarchus.) Because few of the works of Hipparchus have survived, the astronomical ideas in Ptolemy's book are known as the "Ptolemaic system." Ptolemy's system placed the Earth directly at the center of the universe. The Sun, Moon, and planets all orbited the Earth. The observed motions of the planets did not exactly match this scheme, so Ptolemy added small orbits to the planets called epicycles. He then introduced other mathematical devices to make a better fit.

Geocentric theory dominates astronomy

Although the Ptolemaic system was complicated and contained errors, it worked well enough for making fairly accurate predictions of planetary positions. As a result, it was an accepted scientific theory for nearly 1400 years. Nicholas Copernicus was the first astronomer to present a different theory of the universe. In *Revolution of the Heavenly Spheres* (1543) Copernicus claimed that the Sun was the center around which the Earth and other planets rotated. The work of other scientists such as the Danish astronomer Tycho Brahe (see entry) provided further proof that Ptolemy's system was inaccurate. Continuing the work of Brahe, Johannes Kepler (see entry in volume four) discovered that the planets not only travel around the Sun, but they also move in elliptical orbits instead of perfect circles.

Attempts scientific basis of astrology

Although the *Almagest* had a significant impact on science, Ptolemy's work on astrology (the study of the influence of stars and planets on human events) was more popular. In the four-volume *Apotelesmatica,* he attempted to establish astrology as a scientific pursuit. He outlined a system for using observations of heavenly bodies to make large-scale predictions about countries, regions, or societies. Ptolemy also demonstrated how to predict events based on the position of the stars and planets at the time of a person's birth. Because Ptolemy was respected as a scientist, his astrological studies were taken seriously for hundreds of years. While astrology is no longer considered a science, it remains popular throughout the world.

The Formation of the Solar System

The solar system is currently believed to be approximately five billion years old. The Earth and the rest of the solar system formed from an immense cloud of gas and dust. Gravity and rotational forces caused the cloud to flatten into a disc, then much of the cloud's mass drifted into the center of the disc. This material became the Sun. The leftover parts of the cloud formed small bodies called planetesimals. These planetesimals collided with each other, gradually forming larger and larger bodies, some of which became the planets. This process is thought to have taken about twenty-five million years.

Introduces latitude and longitude

Ptolemy is credited with establishing the scientific basis of geography (the scientific study of the Earth). In his eight-volume treatise *Geographike hyphegesis* ("Geography"), he presented a new view of the world based on the idea that the Earth is round. The work included a number of maps depicting what was known of the world from the expeditions of Roman armies. *Geographike hyphegesis* was the first place in which the terms latitude (the distance from equator) and longitude (the distance from an adopted meridian) were used. Ptolemy provided tables of latitude and longitude, explaining how the measurements could be calculated mathematically.

By underestimating the distance around the Earth, however, Ptolemy may have altered the history of the world. After *Geographike hyphegesis* was translated into Latin, Italian explorer Christopher Columbus (1451–1506) accepted Ptolemy's estimate of the size of the Earth and concluded that a shortcut to Asia across the Atlantic was possible.

Ptolemy is thought to have lived into his seventies, but the exact circumstances of his death have never been determined. Although relatively little has been learned about the man himself, his work influenced the greatest debates about the shape and size of the Earth and the universe.

Further Reading

Asimov, Isaac, *Asimov's Biographical Encyclopedia of Science and Technology,* 2nd rev. ed., Doubleday, 1982, pp. 42–43.

Dictionary of Scientific Biography, Volume 11, Scribner's, 1975, pp. 186–206.

Magill, Frank N., editor, *The Great Scientists,* Volume 10, Grolier, 1989, pp. 32–37.

McGraw-Hill Encyclopedia of World Biography, Volume 9, McGraw-Hill, 1973, pp. 33–35.

Walter Reed

Born September 13, 1851
Belroi, Virginia
Died November 23, 1902
Washington, D.C.

Army surgeon and medical researcher Walter Reed helped make the discovery that mosquitoes transmit yellow fever. During his career Reed also made contributions to the control of other deadly diseases, including malaria and typhoid. Although some people questioned Reed's use of humans as test subjects for research, his findings saved thousands of lives. In honor of his efforts to control epidemics, the Army General Hospital in Washington, D.C., was named after Reed.

Becomes army doctor

Reed was born on September 13, 1851, in Belroi, Virginia, to Lemuel Sutton Reed and Pharaba White. In 1869, at the age of eighteen, Reed received a medical degree from the University of Virginia in Charlottesville. The young man then traveled to New York City to pursue further medical studies at Bellevue Hospital. Reed received a second medical degree in 1870. Three years later he served as sanitary inspector for the

Walter Reed was instrumental in determining that the deadly disease yellow fever is carried by mosquitoes.

Portrait: Reproduced by permission of AP/Wide World Photos.

physician and medical researcher Walter Reed played a major role in discovering the causes of some of the most deadly diseases of the late 1800s and early 1900s. As a United States Army surgeon, he served on commissions that investigated outbreaks involving malaria, typhoid, and yellow fever. He is best known for his research on yellow fever during a major epidemic among American troops stationed in Cuba. Reed devised a series of experiments that showed the soldiers were being infected by mosquitoes carrying the disease. His findings led to improved mosquito control, which resulted in an almost total eradication of the disease. Conquering yellow fever allowed the United States to take on numerous projects in tropical areas, including the construction of the Panama Canal.

Brooklyn Board of Health. In 1874, upon receiving a commission as assistant surgeon with the U.S. Army Medical Corps, Reed moved to Arizona. At that time he also married Emilie Lawrence, with whom he had two children. For the next eleven years, Reed worked at military bases in Arizona, Nebraska, Minnesota, and Alabama.

Makes important discoveries

During the 1890s Reed decided to pursue his interest in pathology (the study of disease). Because army bases did not offer appropriate facilities for this kind of research, he applied for a leave of absence to conduct advanced work in pathology. His request was not granted and he was instead transferred to Baltimore, Maryland, to act as attending surgeon. He took a brief clinical course (instruction on the examination of patients) at Johns Hopkins Hospital and met physician William Henry Welch (1850–1934), who opened the first pathology laboratory in the United States. Trained by Welch, Reed refined his medical techniques by conducting experiments and performing autopsies (examinations of dead bodies). He also did work on erysipelas (an acute fibroid disease accompanied by severe skin inflammation) and diphtheria (a contagious disease that causes inflammation of the heart and nervous system and a high fever). Reed's experiments were halted when he was sent to an army outpost at Fort Snelling, Minnesota, where he was promoted to major and made a full surgeon.

When George Sternberg (1838–1915) became the U.S. surgeon general in 1893, Reed returned to Washington as curator (supervisor) of the Army Medical Museum. He also taught courses on bacteriology (the study of disease-causing organisms) and clinical microscopy (the use of, or investigation with, a microscope) at the Army Medical College. During this time Reed made major discoveries and contributions to medical science. When a malaria epidemic broke out at Fort Myer, Virginia, in 1896, he proved that contaminated drinking water was not the cause of the disease, although it was commonly suspected to be the culprit. Reed noted that many areas of Washington, D.C., including the section with the highest rate of infection, drew water from the same source—the Potomac River. He also realized that malaria was striking enlisted men, not officers. The reason, he concluded, was that enlisted men often traveled to the city on a trail that led through a swamp. At first Reed suggested that "bad air" caused the disease, but it was later determined that mosquitoes spread malaria.

Investigates typhoid fever

At the beginning of the Spanish-American War (a brief conflict between Spain and the United States that took place in Cuba in 1898), Reed volunteered to serve in Cuba. To make the best use of his qualifications, however, he was appointed head of a board investigating typhoid fever outbreaks in army camps. (Typhoid fever is a communicable disease caused by a bacterium that produces high fever, headache, and other symptoms.) Hundreds of new cases, many of which proved fatal, were reported each day. In fact, fifty times more soldiers were dying from the epidemic than were being killed in combat.

The bacillus (a rod-shaped bacterium) that caused typhoid was believed to be transmitted by contaminated water. The typhoid board found, however, that it was instead passed by flies and contact with infected feces. The board also discovered that infectious organisms were harbored by carriers (people who are infected but show no signs of the disease). The two-volume report on the typhoid board's investigation is now considered a model for epidemiologists (scientists who study the occurrence and control of disease in a population).

Yellow Fever Halts Construction

The work of physicians Walter Reed and William Gorgas was probably more essential to the completion of the Panama Canal than any engineering methods. Located between the North and South American continents, this man-made waterway connects the Atlantic and Pacific Oceans. In 1881 construction of the canal by the French was halted when more than 20,000 workers died of yellow fever. Before building could be resumed, the United States government insisted that yellow fever and malaria must be controlled. In 1900 Reed was appointed head of the U.S. Army Yellow Fever Board. He conducted experiments that proved the mosquito was a carrier of yellow fever. It was determined that the disease could be controlled through eradication of the insect. In 1904 Gorgas applied mosquito eradication measures to the Canal Zone. By 1906 yellow fever cases had ceased, and the Panama Canal was completed nine years later.

Cause of yellow fever unknown

In 1900 Reed was selected to head an army board that investigated the cause of yellow fever. Commonly referred to as "yellow jack," the disease occurred most often in urban areas and was characterized by hemorrhaging, fever, bloodshot eyes, hiccups, dark-colored vomit, and jaundice (yellow skin). Yellow fever had spread rapidly among army troops in Cuba. In addition, annual outbreaks occurred along the East Coast and in the southern portion of the United States, killing thousands of people. The disease regularly struck the same cities during warm weather, but by late autumn it was gone.

Alabama physician Josiah Nott (1804–1873) had proposed that mosquitoes caused yellow fever, but his evidence was scanty. In 1881 Cuban epidemiologist Carlos Finlay (1833–1915) supported Nott's view, suggesting that the malady was transmitted by *Culex fasciatus* (a mosquito now classified as *Aedes aegypti*). Finlay, however, was not taken seriously. Italian physician Giuseppe Sanarelli (1864–1940) later maintained that a bacterium called *Bacillus icteroides* was the cause of yellow fever.

Reed and American army physician James Carroll (1854–1907) were assigned to investigate Sanarelli's claim, and they proved it was incorrect. A rash of yellow fever soon broke out in Havana, killing thousands of soldiers. Reed traveled to Cuba to head a board of army physicians including Carroll, Jesse W. Lazear (1866–1900), and Aristides Agramonte (1869–1931). The board decided to test the theory that mosquitoes transmitted yellow fever.

Starts experiments on humans

Finlay secured mosquitoes and mosquito eggs that enabled the group to raise the insects. Because animals were not affected by yellow fever, the board decided to use human test subjects. Participants in the study gave their consent and were paid $100. (They would receive an additional $100 if they contracted the disease.) Reed designed and conducted experiments that proved the *Aëdes aegypti* mosquito was a carrier, but not the origin. The board concluded that the female *Aëdes aegypti* mosquito could become a carrier of yellow fever only if it bit a victim during the first three days of the disease. The mosquito was unable to transmit the disease for two weeks, but could remain infectious for up to two months in a warm climate. The board also discovered that having yellow fever made a person immune to further attacks.

During the course of the board's experiments, Lazear was accidentally bitten by an infected mosquito and died twelve days later. He left notes, however, to assist Reed and the others in their experiments. The board induced twenty-two other cases of yellow fever, none of which proved fatal. Carroll became ill with the first experimental case but recovered. Although a vaccination against the disease was not developed until the 1920s, yellow fever was virtually eradicated by 1902 in Cuba through mosquito control.

Honored for work

The board's accomplishment not only saved lives, but also paved the way for ventures into tropical regions throughout the world. For instance, the U.S. government insisted that a method of controlling yellow fever was necessary before construction began on the Panama Canal. Reed earned special recognition for heading the investigation. Harvard University

The Panama Canal. Research conducted by Walter Reed and his colleagues led to the eradication of yellow fever in the canal construction zone. Reproduced by permission of Will and Demi McIntyre. National Audubon Society/Photo Researchers, Inc.

awarded him an honorary master's degree for his work with the yellow fever board. Reed died November 23, 1902, in Washington, D.C., following surgery for a ruptured appendix. The Army General Hospital in Washington, D.C., was later named after Reed.

Further Reading

De Kruif, Paul, *Microbe Hunters,* Harcourt, 1953, pp. 286–307.

Kelly, Howard A., *Walter Reed and Yellow Fever,* 3rd ed., The Norman Remington Company, 1923.

Truby, Albert E., *Memoir of Walter Reed, The Yellow Fever Episode,* P. B. Hoeber, 1943.

"Walter Reed: 'He Gave Man Control of That Dreadful Scourge—Yellow Fever,'" *Archives of Internal Medicine,* Volume 89, pp. 171–87.

Wood, Laura N., *Walter Reed, Doctor in Uniform,* J. Messner, 1943.

Andrei Sakharov

Born May 21, 1921
Moscow, Russia
Died December 14, 1989
Moscow, Russia

Russian physicist Andrei Dmitrievich Sakharov was one of the creators of the hydrogen bomb (a weapon with violent explosive power due to the release of atomic energy; also known as the H-bomb). He was also an outspoken Soviet dissident (a person who rebels against a political system), who called for democratic reform. At first Sakharov was committed to the development of the hydrogen bomb. He believed that equal nuclear strength between the United States and the Soviet Union would prevent a nuclear war. Sakharov eventually changed his mind, however, and fought for nuclear disarmament (the reduced stockpiling of nuclear weapons). In 1980 he was exiled (forcibly sent) to the Russian city of Gorky as punishment. He was later released. In 1975 Sakharov won the Nobel Peace Prize for his attempts to end the arms race.

After developing the hydrogen bomb, Russian physicist Andrei Sakharov promoted human rights and government reform in the Soviet Union.

Studies physics

Sakharov was born in Moscow, Russia, on May 21, 1921, to Dmitri Sakharov and Ekaterina Sofiano. Sakharov taught

Russian physicist Andrei Sakharov was one of the creators of the hydrogen bomb. This weapon was stockpiled by the United States and the Soviet Union during the Cold War. Although Sakharov once believed that equal nuclear strength between the superpowers would ensure peace, he later reversed his position. Sakharov became an outspoken dissident, calling for democratic reform in Russia. His crowning achievement came in 1975 when he won the Nobel Peace Prize. Sakharov's efforts eventually led to nuclear disarmament.

himself to read at the age of four. He read the works of great European, American, and Russian writers such as Charles Dickens, Mark Twain, Jack London, Leo Tolstoy, Aleksander Pushkin, and Nikolai Gogol. The young Sakharov was educated primarily at home, where his father taught him math and physics (the science that deals with matter and energy). A tutor taught him chemistry, biology, history, geography, and Russian. In 1934 Sakharov entered the Third Model School and carried out physics experiments at home.

Sakharov graduated from high school as one of only two honors students in his class. In 1938 he enrolled at Moscow State University and studied physics. When Germany invaded the Soviet Union in 1941, Sakharov began working for the war effort. During World War II (1939–1945), he repaired radio equipment and invented a magnetic device for locating shrapnel (metal fragments) in injured horses. After graduating in 1942, Sakharov left the university to devote his time to the war effort. While working at a cartridge factory in Ulyanovsk, Russia, he devised a new method of testing armor-piercing bullets for antitank guns.

Works on hydrogen bomb

In 1945 Sakharov joined the staff of the P. N. Lebedev Institute of Physics of the Soviet Academy of Science. At the academy he worked with the Nobel Prize-winning Russian physicist Igor Tamm (1895–1971). Sakharov produced papers on the generation of cosmic rays (small particles traveling through space), the interaction of electrons and positrons (the antimatter equivalent of electrons), and plasma (a collection of charged particles). In 1948 Sakharov and Tamm published a paper outlining a principle for the magnetic isolation of

Nuclear Winter

The Cold War began in 1946 and lasted into the late 1980s. During this time, the United States and the former Soviet Union stockpiled many nuclear weapons. Due to this stockpile and ongoing hostilities between the two countries, people all over the world believed that nuclear war could break out at any moment. This fear led many researchers to wonder what the consequences of such a disaster would be. Scientists coined the term "nuclear winter" to describe the potentially horrendous results. They speculated that nuclear war would lead to prolonged periods of darkness, below-freezing temperatures, violent windstorms, and persistent radioactive fallout. The atmosphere of the entire northern hemisphere would contain a blanket of ash so thick that very little sunlight would reach the earth. Since the collapse of the Soviet Union and the end of the Cold War, politicians and scientists have worked to dismantle the world's nuclear arsenal and end the threat of nuclear winter.

high temperature plasma. This work changed the entire course of Soviet thermonuclear physics (the science of transforming the nucleus of atoms of low atomic weight under very high temperatures).

After publishing their revolutionary work, Sakharov and Tamm disappeared from the general scientific community for twenty years. The two men had been selected to work on a hydrogen bomb. In 1948 they were transferred with the rest of the H-bomb team to the Installation, a secret city where the bomb project was carried out. In 1950 Sakharov and Tamm developed a theoretical basis for controlled thermonuclear fusion. (Fusion is the union of atomic nuclei to form heavier nuclei resulting in the release of enormous quantities of energy when light elements unite.) Instead of using nuclear power only for weapons, the researchers devised a method of employing it for peaceful means, such as the generation of electricity. Despite this discovery, most of the work at the Installation was geared toward the violent use of nuclear energy.

By 1953 the H-bomb team was ready to carry out the first test explosion of a Soviet hydrogen bomb. Although the

United States had already tested an H-bomb, the Soviets were the first country to explode a compact device that could be delivered by plane or rocket. Sakharov was credited with developing a triggering mechanism that used a fission explosion to set off the process of hydrogen fusion, which then released the bomb's destructive energy.

Becomes a dissident

By the end of the 1950s Sakharov was questioning the morality of some of his scientific work. For the next three decades he was actively involved in protests against the hydrogen bomb. He began with an unsuccessful attempt to end the government's plan to resume nuclear testing. In the 1960s Sakharov abandoned thermonuclear science to study the universe and to write about political subjects. In 1968 he published his manifesto (statement of political views), called *Reflections on Progress, Coexistence, and Intellectual Freedom.* In the essay he discussed nuclear annihilation and proposed a peaceful solution that would blend socialism (a theory advocating collective or government ownership of the means of production and distribution of goods) and capitalism (private ownership of goods and distribution of goods in a free market).

In 1968 Sakharov completely abandoned the military-industrial complex when the Soviet Union invaded Czechoslovakia, a country that was becoming democratic (adopting a government elected by the vote of the people). In 1970 Sakharov and other Soviet scientists formed the Committee for Human Rights to promote the principles of the Universal Declaration of Human Rights. His "Manifesto II" was also published that year in the form of an open address to Soviet President Leonid Brezhnev (1906–1982). Sakharov won the Nobel Peace Prize in 1975, but he was not allowed to travel to Norway to accept the honor.

Sent into exile

In 1979 Sakharov became especially vocal in his opposition to the Soviet invasion of Afghanistan (a country on the southern border of the former Soviet Union). As a result, in 1980 he was exiled to the isolated Russian town of Gorky and kept under constant surveillance. On November 21, 1981, Sakharov began a seventeen-day hunger strike that attracted worldwide attention. He staged two more hunger strikes in 1984 and 1985. Finally, on December 16, 1986, Sakharov was released from exile. In 1988 he traveled abroad for the first time in his life. In the United States he met President George Bush (1924–). He also visited France, Italy, and Canada.

Receives awards and honors

Before Sakharov abandoned his scientific career, he was richly rewarded for his work on the hydrogen bomb. In 1953 he became the youngest man to be elected a full member of the Soviet Academy of Sciences. He was also given a modest salary and better housing than most Soviet citizens. Sakharov is perhaps best known, however, for the political activities that won him universal acclaim. He was elected a foreign member of the American Academy of Arts and Sciences in 1969 and a member of the National Academy of Sciences in 1972. He received the Eleanor Roosevelt Peace Award from SANE (Committee for a Sane Nuclear Policy; 1973). He was also named a foreign associate of the French Academy of Science (1981).

In 1943 Sakharov married Klavdia (Klava) Vikhireva, with whom he had three children. Klavdia died of cancer in 1969. Two years later Sakharov married Yelena Bonner (1923–), an Armenian-Siberian Jewish dissident. Sakharov himself died of a heart attack on December 14, 1989, in Moscow.

Further Reading

Babyonyshev, Alexander, editor, *On Sakharov,* Knopf, 1982.

Bonner, Yelena, *Alone Together,* Knopf, 1986.

Medvedev, Zhores A., *Soviet Science,* Norton, 1978.

Parry, Albert, *The Russian Scientist,* Macmillan, 1973, p. 172.

Sakharov, Andrei, *Memoirs,* Knopf, 1990.

Nettie Maria Stevens

Born July 7, 1861
Cavendish, Vermont
Died May 4, 1912

Nettie Maria Stevens discovered that the gender of an organism is determined by an inherited chromosome.

Portrait: Reproduced by permission of the Science Photo Library/Photo Researchers, Inc.

Biologist Nettie Maria Stevens conducted research on chromosomes (DNA-containing bodies of virus), making an important contribution to the new field of genetics (the science of heredity). Building on the ideas of Austrian monk Gregor Mendel (see entry in volume two), Stevens proposed that the gender of an organism is determined according to specific genetic rules. She believed that the sex of an organism is determined by the inheritance of a specific X or Y chromosome. Performing experiments to confirm her belief, Stevens found that in animals the cell donated by the female always contains the X chromosome. The cell donated by the male, however, can carry either an X or a Y chromosome. When the male contributes an X chromosome, the offspring is female. When the Y chromosome is present, the offspring is male. Even though Stevens's theory was not widely accepted at the time, it was an important step forward in the field of genetics.

Returns to college at late age

Stevens was born in Cavendish, Vermont, on July 7, 1861, to Ephraim and Julia Adams Stevens. She was educated in the public schools in Westford, Massachusetts. After graduating from high school, she taught a variety of subjects, including math and science, at the high school in Lebanon, New Hampshire. Between 1881 and 1883 Stevens attended the Normal School (a teacher's college) at Westfield, Massachusetts. Upon completing college she spent a number of years working as a school teacher and a librarian. During this period, however, Stevens never lost her desire to learn. In 1896, at the age of thirty-five, she enrolled at Stanford University in California, once again becoming a student.

At the time Stanford students were allowed to pursue independent study, and this approach to learning appealed to Stevens. After deciding to change her focus from teaching to scientific research, she began studying physiology (the branch of biology that deals with the functions of life or living matter). In order to obtain practical experience in biological research, Stevens spent her summers at the Hopkins Seaside Laboratory in Pacific Grove, California. While at Hopkins she investigated the life cycle of Boveria (a microscopic parasite that preys on sea cucumbers). Her findings were published in 1901 in the proceedings of the California Academy of Sciences.

After obtaining a master's degree—a highly unusual accomplishment for a woman in that era—Stevens returned to the east coast. In 1900 she entered Bryn Mawr College in Pennsylvania as a graduate student in biology. Stevens was awarded a fellowship that enabled her to study at the Zoological Station in Naples, Italy, and at the Zoological Institute of the University of Würzburg, Germany. After returning to Bryn Mawr, Stevens received a doctorate in 1903. She then stayed

≋IMPACT≋

Nettie Maria Stevens was one of the first American women to be recognized for making contributions to scientific research. Although Stevens began her career late in life, she made important discoveries in the field of genetics. Her research provided new information about chromosomes, including the first evidence that chromosomes play a role in the inheritance of specific traits. This finding inspired other scientists, including 1933 Nobel Prize-winner Thomas Hunt Morgan, to further develop the science of genetics.

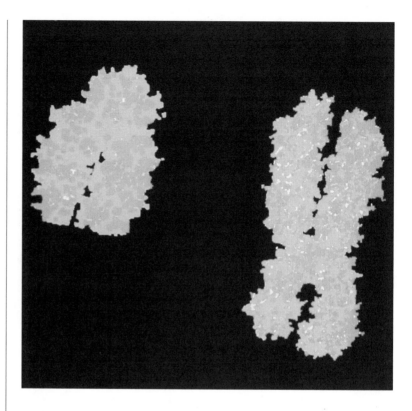

at the college as a research fellow in biology. She was promoted to instructor the following year. Stevens remained at Bryn Mawr until her death in 1912.

Shifts research focus

When Stevens began her research she focused on morphology (a branch of biology that deals with the form and structure of plants) and taxonomy (the scientific classification of organisms). She later expanded her investigation to cytology (the study of structures and activities within cells). Stevens's most important research, however, was on chromosomes and their relation to heredity (the inheritance of traits). The study of heredity had been pioneered by Mendel, who had conducted experiments that showed how genetic traits are inherited in pea plants. Because of his work, scientists knew how chromosomes act during cell division and in the maturation of cells. However, no inherited trait had been traced from the parents' chromosomes to those of the offspring. In addition, no scientific studies had yet linked a particular chromosome with a specific characteristic.

Makes chromosome discoveries

Working with the *Tenebrio molitor,* or mealworm, Stevens found that the male produced two kinds of sperm (male fluid that fertilizes a female egg)—one with a large X chromosome and the other with a small Y chromosome. Yet unfertilized eggs were identical and all had the X chromosome. Stevens theorized that sex, in some organisms, may result from chromosomal inheritance. She suggested that eggs fertilized by sperm that carry an X chromosome produce females, and those by sperm that carry a Y chromosome result in males. Stevens performed further research to prove this phenomenon, expanding her studies to other species.

Stevens's theory was not accepted by all scientists at the time. Nevertheless, it was profoundly important in the evolution of the field of genetics and, eventually, to an understanding of how gender is determined. Much later Thomas Hunt Morgan (see entry), a 1933 Nobel Prize winner for work in genetics, recognized the importance of the experiments conducted by Stevens.

Edmund Beecher Wilson

Nettie Maria Stevens and Edmund Beecher Wilson independently demonstrated that the sex of an organism is determined by a particular chromosome. During his career Wilson emphasized careful experimentation and analysis in biology. His work was instrumental in transforming the field into a rigorous scientific discipline. Wilson's influence was felt through his position as a professor—first at Bryn Mawr College and then at Columbia University—and through his textbook, *The Cell in Development and Inheritance* (1896). Wilson's research on chromosomes, and especially his discovery of the sex chromosomes, helped lay the foundation for the study of genetics and evolution in the early twentieth century. Many of the problems Wilson tackled, including the details of cell development, remain unsolved today.

Confirms basis for heredity

Stevens and biologist Edmund Beecher Wilson (1856–1939) independently demonstrated that the sex of an organism is determined by a particular chromosome. This research confirmed a chromosomal basis for heredity. During her career Stevens was a productive author, publishing around thirty-eight papers in eleven years. From 1903 until 1905 her research was funded by a grant from the Carnegie Institute. For her paper titled "A Study of the Germ Cells of Aphis rosae and Aphis oenotherae," Stevens was awarded the Ellen Richards Research Prize (awarded to promote scientific research by women) in 1905. Stevens died of breast cancer on May 4, 1912, before she could occupy the research professorship created for her by the Bryn Mawr College trustees.

Further Reading

Isis, June 1978, pp. 163–72.

Ogilvie, Marilyn Bailey, *Women in Science: Antiquity through the Nineteenth Century,* MIT Press, 1986.

Proceedings of the American Philosophical Society, Held at Philadelphia for Promoting Useful Knowledge, Volume 125, American Philosophical Society, 1981, pp. 292–311.

Leo Szilard

Born February 11, 1898
Budapest, Hungary
Died May 30, 1964
La Jolla, California

Hungarian-born physicist Leo Szilard was one of the leading contributors to the development of nuclear energy and atomic weapons in the United States. He was also among the earliest and most active campaigners for nuclear arms control. As a member of the Manhattan Project in 1942, he set up the first nuclear chain reaction with Italian physicist Enrico Fermi (1901–1954). This work led to the successful creation of the atomic bombs used in World War II (1939–1945) against Japan. In addition to his work with nuclear energy, Szilard made other contributions to science. For instance, he wrote his doctoral thesis on entropy (a measure of the unavailable energy in a system). He also studied X–ray crystallography (the use of X rays to examine the atomic structure of crystals) and worked with particle accelerators (machines used to increase the speed of subatomic particles). After the war Szilard began studying and teaching biophysics (the application of physics to biology).

Leo Szilard made important contributions to the early understanding and use of nuclear energy.

Portrait: Reproduced by permission of the Library of Congress.

Hungarian-born physicist Leo Szilard devised the concept of a nuclear chain reaction. This powerful new force was put to use in World War II, when the United States rushed to develop atomic bombs via the Manhattan Project. Szilard played a key role in this undertaking, working with Enrico Fermi to set up the first chain reaction in 1942. The successful creation of nuclear weapons allowed the United States to quickly end the war by dropping atomic bombs on Hiroshima and Nagasaki in Japan in 1945. After the war Szilard worked to find peaceful uses for nuclear fission by advocating an end to the stockpiling of nuclear weapons by the United States and the Soviet Union.

Called into army

Szilard was born in Budapest, Hungary, on February 11, 1898. He was the son of Louis Szilard, an architect and engineer, and Thekla (Vidor) Szilard. In 1916, at the age of eighteen, Szilard entered the Budapest Institute of Technology to study electrical engineering. At the end of his first year, he was called to serve in the Austro-Hungarian army and assigned to officer training school. He became very ill, however, and had not fully recovered by the end of World War I (1914–1918). He returned to the Budapest Institute of Technology before transferring to the Technische Hochschule at Berlin-Charlottenburg in Germany.

Influenced by leading physicists

In Berlin, Szilard came into contact with some of the finest physicists in the world, including Albert Einstein (see entry in volume one), Max Planck (see entry in volume three), and Max von Laue (1879–1960). Szilard decided that his real interest lay in physics (the science of matter and energy) rather than engineering. He then began a course of study with von Laue as his doctoral adviser. In 1922 Szilard received a Ph.D., having written his doctoral thesis on the second law of thermodynamics (the concept that the energy in a closed system will eventually run down through the release of heat; also called entropy).

Szilard's work on entropy continued for a number of years, culminating in a paper titled "On the Decrease of Entropy in a Thermodynamic System by the Intervention of Intelligent Beings" (1929). In the paper he applied thermodynamics (the branch of physics dealing with the mechanics of heat) to information theory (a concept that deals with statistical measurement of information and effective processes of communication). Szilard's work is regarded as an important precursor to modern cybernetics (the study of intelligent communication and control systems).

Expands to new areas

After receiving his degree, Szilard was appointed a research assistant at the Institute of Theoretical Physics at the University of Berlin. In 1925 he became a Privatdozent (instructor) at the institute, which was headed by von Laue. In addition to continuing his work on thermodynamics, Szilard began a series of studies on X-ray crystallography, a field in which von Laue was a world leader. Szilard also worked closely with Einstein on the development of a pump for liquid metals, for which he eventually obtained a patent (a government grant giving an inventor the sole rights to manufacture and sell an invention). In addition, he became interested in the problem of particle accelerators (machines used to increase the speed of subatomic particles). Szilard invented a number of devices that were later to be incorporated into early cyclotrons, which are particle accelerators designed to speed up protons and ions (atoms or molecules from which electrons have been removed).

Invents nuclear chain reaction

In 1933, the rise of German Nazi leader Adolf Hitler (1889–1945) convinced Szilard, who was Jewish, to flee from Germany to England. (The Nazi Party initiated a series of harsh policies in Germany, including the repression of Jews.) After arriving in England, Szilard received news of the discovery of artificial radioactivity by French physicists Frédéric Joliot-Curie and Irène Joliot-Curie (see joint entry in volume four). (Radioactivity is a phenomenon in which the atomic nucleus of certain elements releases small charged particles. Radioactivity naturally occurs in some elements, such as radium and polonium.) The Joliot-Curies found that other naturally stable elements, such as aluminum, could be made radioactive by bombarding them with alpha particles (one of the types of particles released from radioactive materials). The alpha particles would add protons to the atomic nucleus, resulting in an unstable form of a new element. An atom of aluminum, for example, would be changed into a radioactive isotope (a form of an element with the same atomic number, but a different atomic mass) of phosphorus.

Upon hearing of this discovery, Szilard began to think about the possibility of a nuclear chain reaction. According to Szilard's theory, the nuclear decay of one atom would be brought about by some type of particle. As a result, a new atom would be produced with the release of more particles of the kind needed to start the reaction. Once the reaction was started, it would be self-sustaining over many, many episodes of decay. Szilard knew that the value of such a reaction was that energy would be released in each step of the process. Countless repetitions of the reaction would release huge amounts of energy—sufficient, for instance, to make a powerful bomb.

Beryllium experiment fails

Szilard explored the possibility of using beryllium (a strong, toxic metallic element used in alloys) in such a chain reaction. He and a colleague named T. A. Chalmers found that gamma rays (another type of energy released by radioactive material) directed at a beryllium target would cause the release of a neutron (an atomic particle with mass, but no charge) from the beryllium nucleus. The scientists hoped this reaction could act as the first step in a chain reaction in which beryllium atoms would break apart to form helium atoms and more neutrons. The neutrons would then cause more beryllium atoms to break apart into helium atoms with the release of more neutrons, and so on. More detailed studies showed, however, that such a reaction could not be sustained.

Fission solves problem

Toward the end of 1938, Szilard decided to move to the United States to work at Columbia University in New York

City. As soon as he arrived, Szilard received startling news from Europe. German chemists Otto Hahn (1879–1968) and Fritz Strassman (1902–1980) had produced the first fission (splitting) of an atomic nucleus, an event that was explained by Austrian physicist Lise Meitner (see entry in volume two) in 1939. Szilard immediately recognized the significance of this discovery. It could potentially produce the very kind of nuclear chain reaction he had been working on in London.

With Canadian-American physicist Walter Zinn (1906–), Szilard set up a replica of the Hahn–Strassman experiment at Columbia. The scientists' goal was to find out whether the fission of a uranium nucleus would result in the formation of at least one neutron, a condition necessary for the maintenance of a chain reaction. On March 3, 1939, the experiment was ready. A few flashes of light on an oscilloscope (an instrument designed to measure changes in energy levels) gave Szilard and Zinn the answer they sought—neutrons were being released during the fission of uranium atoms. A nuclear chain reaction was possible. News of this achievement swept like wildfire through the physics community. Szilard later said he knew immediately that this discovery would cause the world great sorrow.

"The Shatterer of Worlds"

Physicist Leo Szilard took part in the first major accomplishment of the Manhattan Project, a self-sustaining nuclear chain reaction, on December 2, 1942. Three years later an atomic bomb was built. The first experimental bomb was exploded in a desert area near Alamogordo, New Mexico, on July, 16, 1945. The test site was called Trinity, and the bomb generated an explosive power equivalent to between 15,000 and 20,000 tons of TNT. After witnessing the test, project scientists were overwhelmed by the force they had created. Physicist J. Robert Oppenheimer (see entry in volume two), remarking on the extreme brightness of the explosion, quoted a line from the great Hindu work, *Bhagavad-Gita:* "I am become death, the Shatterer of Worlds."

Leads effort for bomb project

Many scientists, who understood the potential military uses of nuclear fission, were concerned that Germany might develop atomic weapons. They were convinced that the U.S. government had to take fast and aggressive action. Szilard composed a letter, which Einstein signed, urging President

Franklin D. Roosevelt (1882–1945) to investigate the use of nuclear fission. In June 1942 the Manhattan Project was created to build atomic bombs. That same year Szilard joined the project at the University of Chicago. Working with Fermi, he witnessed a controlled nuclear reaction on December 2, 1942, when the world's first nuclear reactor was put into operation.

Fights development of nuclear weapons

Shortly after this landmark event, Szilard began to argue for an end to research on nuclear weapons. A number of factors influenced his position, including the realization that horrible human tragedies would result from the explosion of an atomic bomb. He suggested that the United States invite Japanese government officials to a demonstration of nuclear weapons in an uninhabited area. After witnessing the catastrophic explosion, he reasoned, they would surrender. Szilard's idea fell on deaf ears. In August 1945, atomic bombs were dropped on the cities of Hiroshima and Nagasaki in Japan. World War II ended a week later.

Advocates nuclear disarmament

In the years following World War II, Szilard campaigned for the control of the frightening force he had helped release. He joined many other nuclear physicists in forming the Federation of Atomic Scientists. The organization worked to keep control of atomic energy out of the hands of the military and within a civilian department. Szilard also made efforts to encourage mutual disarmament (the reduction of weapons) and the easing of tensions between the United States and the Soviet Union. He was also actively involved the Pugwash Conferences on Science and World Affairs, a series of meetings on nuclear safety that took place in the late 1950s and early 1960s. In 1962 he helped found the Council for a Livable World, an organization based in Washington, D.C., that was created to lobby for nuclear arms control.

Honored for peace efforts

In the late 1940s, Szilard began studying biology. After becoming a U.S. citizen in 1943, he taught biophysics (the application of physics to biology) at the University of Chicago. In 1951 he married Gertrud Weiss, a medical student from Vienna, Austria. Szilard was awarded the Einstein Gold Medal in 1958 and the Atoms for Peace Award in 1959. He died of a heart attack on May 30, 1964, in La Jolla, California.

Further Reading

Coffin, Tristram, "Leo Szilard: The Conscience of a Scientist," *Holiday,* February 1964.

McGraw-Hill Modern Scientists and Engineers, Volume 10, McGraw-Hill, 1980, pp. 181–82.

Szilard, Leo, *Collected Words of Leo Szilard,* edited by Bernard T. Feld and Gertrud W. Szilard, MIT Press, 1972.

Szilard, Leo, *Leo Szilard: His Version of the Facts: Selected Recollections and Correspondence,* edited by Spencer R. Weart and Gertrud W. Szilard, MIT Press, 1978.

Wigner, Eugene, "Leo Szilard, 1898–1964," *Biographical Memoirs: National Academy of Sciences,* Volume 40, 1969, pp. 337–41.

Karen E. Wetterhahn

Born in 1948
Plattsburgh, New York
Died June 8, 1997
Hanover, New Hampshire

Karen Wetterhahn was a chemistry professor at Dartmouth College in Hanover, New Hampshire, where she conducted environmental research projects. During an experiment in August 1996, Wetterhahn was employing a method of nuclear magnetic resonance (NMR) spectroscopy (the use of an instrument called a spectroscope to form and examine the visible region of the electromagnetic spectrum). Part of her experiment involved working with dimethyl mercury (a highly toxic chemical). At one point Wetterhahn spilled a tiny amount of the chemical on her hands. She died six months later. Ironically, Wetterhahn's objective had been to determine the effects that heavy metals (such as mercury) produce on the environment. This accident sparked a national debate about the risks involved in chemical research.

Begins working at Dartmouth College

Wetterhahn was born in Plattsburgh, New York, in 1948. In 1970 she graduated magna cum laude (with high honors) from St. Lawrence University in Canton, New York. Five years later she received a doctoral degree from Columbia University in New York City. In 1976 Wetterhahn joined the faculty of Dartmouth College in Hanover, New Hampshire. At Dartmouth she initiated a curriculum in structural biology (a field of science that studies biologically active molecules). In August 1996 Wetterhahn was conducting an experiment to determine the effect that heavy metals (which include mercury, chromium, lead, and arsenic) have on living things.

Uses most toxic compound

In order to carry out the experiment, Wetterhahn used NMR to examine the binding of mercury to a protein that is involved in the repair of DNA. (DNA, deoxyribonucleic acid, is a substance present in the nucleus of every cell that determines individual characteristics.) During the procedure, Wetterhahn measured the resonance (alternation) of the bound mercury nuclei (plural for nucleus, the center of a cell) to determine what part of the protein was being attacked. After measuring the resonance, she compared it to a compound that contains the element.

As the standard (basis) for her comparison, Wetterhahn chose dimethyl mercury. (Dimethyl is derived from a colorless and highly flammable substance called methane; mercury is a silver-white, heavy metallic element in liquid form.) Dimethyl mercury belongs to the methylmercury group of compounds, which is the most toxic (poisonous) form. It crosses the blood-brain barrier (seeps from the bloodstream into brain tissues) and causes fatal damage to the central nervous system and the brain. Symptoms of mercury poisoning include loss of motor (movement) control, numbness in the arms and legs, blindness, and inability to speak.

IMPACT

Dartmouth College professor Karen Wetterhahn died of mercury poisoning on June 8, 1997, six months after a laboratory accident involving dimethyl mercury, a highly toxic chemical. Two months later the Occupational Safety and Health Administration (OSHA) fined Dartmouth for not informing researchers about the dangers of using latex gloves with certain toxic materials. Dartmouth responded by placing warning stickers on boxes of latex gloves and by alerting other schools about the dangers of dimethyl mercury. College officials also instituted workshops to educate faculty and staff about potential dangers in the laboratory. Finally, OSHA urged the scientific community to use a less dangerous chemical such as inorganic mercury salt, which is less likely to permeate the skin.

Mercury Poisoning

Scientists have long been aware that mercury is highly poisonous, but the most significant research on the subject was not done until the mid-twentieth century. Mercury was known to the ancient Chinese, Hindus, and Egyptians. It was used as a medicine by the sixteenth-century German alchemist and physician Paracelsus (Phillipus Bombast von Hohenheim; 1493–1541). During the nineteenth century, when mercury was used in the manufacture of felt hats, the phrase "mad as a hatter" was applied to workers who suffered from prolonged contact with the element. Since mercury is not easily discharged from the body, poisoning takes place slowly. Symptoms include skin eruptions, bleeding gums, trembling hands, digestive disorders, kidney ailments, liver disease, and deafness. Mercury is a serious threat to the environment, causing the pollution of rivers, lakes, and oceans. Scientists have discovered that heavy mercury concentrations can contaminate fish and other sea life that is used for food. As a result, ninety-one countries banned the ocean dumping of mercury and other polluting substances in 1972.

Has fatal accident

During her experiment Wetterhahn was transferring some dimethyl mercury to an NMR tube when she spilled a tiny amount of the toxic compound on her hands. Even though she was wearing latex (synthetic rubber or plastic) gloves, the clear liquid permeated the thin layer of latex and seeped into her skin within seconds. Wetterhahn did not feel the effects of the exposure until six months later, when she began losing her balance, slurring her speech, and suffering vision and hearing loss. Tests revealed that there was more than eighty times the lethal dose of mercury in her system. Wetterhahn died of mercury poisoning on June 8, 1997, less than a year after the accident.

OSHA cites Dartmouth

On August 18, 1997, the U.S. Occupational Safety and Health Administration (OSHA) fined Dartmouth College $13,500 for its role in Wetterhahn's death. The agency ruled that the college had not warned its researchers about the limitations of latex gloves. As Wetterhahn's death demonstrated, the gloves do not adequately protect the skin from deadly compounds such as dimethyl mercury. Chemists found that this compound permeates disposable gloves in fifteen seconds or less. OSHA also cited Dartmouth for not supplying other types of protection besides latex gloves. OSHA suggested that scientists wear highly resistant laminate gloves (consisting of several bonded layers) under a pair of heavy-duty neoprene gloves. (Neoprene is a synthetic rubber that is highly resistant to oils and other substances. It is also used to make wet suits.) The safety agency recommended that scientists wear these stronger gloves especially when handling compounds such as dimethyl mercury.

A mercury waste landfill site. Dr. Karen Wetterhahn conducted experiments to determine how chemicals like mercury affected the environment. Reproduced by permission of Recio/Greenpeace.

Dartmouth makes changes

Dartmouth responded to the Wetterhahn tragedy by placing brightly colored warning stickers on boxes of latex gloves, alerting users that the gloves are not intended for use with hazardous chemicals. Dartmouth officials also warned other schools and laboratories about the dangers of dimethyl mercury and other dangerous materials. Finally, the college instituted workshops to educate faculty and staff about proper glove selection.

As a part of a national safety crusade, OSHA urged the scientific community to use a less dangerous chemical than dimethyl mercury in research. Researchers who practice NMR spectroscopy have traditionally preferred dimethyl mercury because it produces a clear NMR signal. They can also use inorganic mercury salt, however, which is much safer. Since the compound is a solid rather than a liquid, scientists face less chance of inhaling or absorbing deadly mercury.

Left valuable legacy

Even though Wetterhahn became quite famous after her death, she was also respected during her lifetime. She was the author of more than eighty-five research papers and a member of several scientific societies. She was an Alfred P. Sloan Fellow (1981–1985) and she cofounded the Women in Science Project in order to increase the number of women participating in science. Wetterhahn was survived by her husband and two children.

For Further Reading

"An Avoidable Tragedy," *Occupational Hazards,* August, 1997.

"Colleagues Vow to Learn from Chemist's Death," *New York Times,* October 3, 1997.

Nancy Wexler

Born July 19, 1945
Washington, D.C.

E ver since her mother was diagnosed with Huntington's disease in 1968, researcher Nancy Sabin Wexler has been active in efforts to understand and cure the disease. She studied a community in Venezuela (a South American country) with a high rate of the deadly genetic disorder, then helped to organize the Huntington's Disease Research Collaborative Group in 1984. These efforts led to the development of a test for the genetic condition before symptoms appear. Continued research resulted in the landmark discovery, in 1993, of the exact gene that causes Huntington's disease. For her important role in these achievements, Wexler was granted the highest honor in American medicine, the Albert Lasker Public Service Award.

Nancy Wexler has led the search for answers about Huntington's disease, a fatal genetic disorder.

Begins investigating Huntington's

Wexler was born on July 19, 1945, in Washington, D.C. Her parents, Milton Wexler and Leonore Sabin Wexler, were

Psychologist and medical researcher Nancy Wexler has led efforts to understand Huntington's disease, a deadly genetic disorder for which she herself is at risk. Wexler worked with the federal government to provide scientific funding for efforts to learn more about the disorder. In 1981 she began collecting blood samples and other data from a community in Venezuela that had a high rate of Huntington's disease. The blood samples led to the discovery of a genetic marker that could determine if a patient had inherited the condition. To help scientists pinpoint the exact location of the gene that causes Huntington's, Wexler founded the Huntington's Disease Collaborative Research Group in 1984. The group succeeded in locating the Huntington's gene in 1993, achieving a breakthrough in research on genetic disorders.

divorced in 1964. In 1967 Wexler graduated with honors from Radcliffe College in Massachusetts, where she studied social relations and English. The following year Wexler reached a turning point in her career when she learned from her father that her mother had Huntington's disease. The symptoms of this fatal disorder usually appear around middle age, and the disease leads to the eventual degeneration of mental and physical functioning. Milton Wexler also informed his daughter that there was a 50 percent chance that she herself had inherited the gene (a functional unit of inheritance) that causes the disease. Although the news was distressing, it answered many of Wexler's questions about her family. She now knew that the mysterious deaths of her mother's father and three brothers had been due to Huntington's.

Wexler has credited her father with being her inspiration in battling the disease. Soon after his former wife was diagnosed with the disorder, he became involved with an organization called The Committee to Combat Huntington's Chorea. The group was founded by the widow of folk singer Woody Guthrie (1912–1967), who had died of the disease. Milton Wexler formed a California chapter of the committee, which focused on encouraging scientists to research Huntington's. When Nancy Wexler entered the University of Michigan in Ann Arbor to study clinical psychology, she formed a Michigan chapter of the organization.

In addition to her work to raise awareness about Huntington's disease, Wexler focused her career on investigating the deadly condition. She wrote her doctoral thesis on the "Perceptual-motor, Cognitive, and Emotional Characteristics of

Persons-at-Risk for Huntington's Disease." After receiving a Ph.D. from the University of Michigan in 1974, Wexler taught psychology at the New School for Social Research in New York City. She also worked as a researcher on Huntington's disease for the National Institutes of Health (NIH). In 1976 she was appointed by the U.S. Congress to head the NIH Commission for the Control of Huntington's Disease and Its Consequences.

When her mother died in 1978, Wexler became even more determined to learn more about the disorder. In 1983 she took over leadership of the Hereditary Disease Foundation, an organization formed by her father. In 1985 she joined the College of Physicians and Surgeons at Columbia University as a professor and clinical psychologist.

Genetic marker discovered

In her role as head of the NIH Huntington's disease commission, Wexler fought for federal funding to study the disorder. When financial support was finally approved in 1977, she started a research project in Venezuela. In 1979 Wexler went to Lake Maracaibo, Venezuela, where a high concentration of Huntington's patients lived. In 1981 she began conducting annual information-gathering expeditions to the region. Wexler kept medical records, took blood and skin samples, and charted the transmission of Huntington's disease within families.

Wexler sent the blood samples to geneticist James Gusella at the Massachusetts General Hospital. Gusella used the samples to conduct a study to estimate the general location of the Huntington's gene. Gusella eventually discovered a

Joins Human Genome Project

As a result of her pioneering research on Huntington's disease, medical researcher Nancy Wexler was invited to join the Human Genome Project. This multi-billion-dollar program began in 1990, when the biomedical community decided to map the entire human genome (the complete genetic structure of a species) which involves locating 70,000 genes. The goal is not only to pinpoint these genes, but also to decode the biochemical information down to "letters" of inheritance. Representing the four basic constituents of all genes, which are called nucleotides, the letters are A (adenine), C (cytosine), G (guanine), and T (thymine). Since the letters are linked in pairs of sequences in the double helix of DNA, this means that three billion pairs are involved in the process. By 1998 approximately 4 percent of the human genome had been sequenced.

unique deoxyribonucleic acid (DNA) structure—called a marker—that was linked to the Huntington's gene. This marker always appeared in the same chromosome (DNA-containing body of virus), which meant that for the first time scientists were able to locate a specific gene. In 1982, on the basis of this study, Gusella introduced a test that was 96 percent accurate in detecting whether an individual bears the Huntington's gene. Because there was still no cure for Huntington's disease, however, the test proved to be controversial. It raised many issues involving patient rights, childbearing decisions, and discrimination by employers and insurance companies.

Narrowing down the location of the Huntington's gene was a major breakthrough. Nevertheless, Wexler and other scientists felt that the exact gene needed to be identified before the disease could be cured. In order to ensure that such research was conducted with cooperation and efficiency, Wexler formed the Huntington's Disease Collaborative Research Group in 1984. Under this collective name, she gathered together more than fifty scientists working at six different laboratories in the United States and Europe. Wexler's leadership eventually paid off in 1993, when the Huntington's gene was identified through research based on the Venezuelan blood samples and the work of the Huntington's Disease Collaborative Research Group. Wexler and her colleagues realized they had made an important discovery, which might someday lead to treatments and cures.

Receives highest honor

As a result of her pioneering work in identifying the Huntington's gene, Wexler was invited to serve as an adviser on social and medical ethics issues related to the Human Genome Project. (This project is a massive international effort to map and identify the approximately 70,000 genes in the human body.) During the 1990s Wexler continued to lead research with the Huntington's Disease Collaborative Research Group. Since the discovery of the Huntington's gene, the organization has worked to find out why the disease affects only certain parts of the brain. Wexler also continued to conduct research in Venezuela, where she identified the original ancestor of all the Huntington's patients in the Lake Maracaibo area. In 1993 Wexler received an Albert Lasker Public Service Award for her research of Huntington's disease.

Further Reading

"An Array of New Tools against Inherited Diseases," *U.S. News & World Report,* April 22, 1985, pp. 75–76.

Bluestone, Mimi, "Science and Ethics: The Double Life of Nancy Wexler," *Ms.,* November/December 1991, pp. 90–91.

Grady, Denise, "The Ticking of a Time Bomb in the Genes," *Discover,* June 1987.

Jaroff, Leon, "Making the Best of a Bad Gene," *Time,* February 10, 1992, pp. 78–79.

Konner, Melvin, "New Keys to the Mind," *The New York Times Magazine,* July 17, 1988, pp. 49–50.

Newsmakers, Gale, 1992, pp. 530–33.

New York Times, October 1, 1993, p. A24.

Revkin, Andrew, "Hunting Down Huntington's," *Discover,* December 1993, pp. 98–108.

Cumulative Index to Volumes 1-6

Italic type indicates volume numbers; **boldface** type indicates entries and their page numbers; (ill.) indicates illustrations.

Nancy Wexler.
Reproduced by permission
of the Library of Congress.

Alvarez, Luis *1:* **7–14,** 7 (ill.),
11 (ill.)
Alvarez, Walter *1:* 9, 13
Alvariño, Angeles *1:* **15–18**
Alzheimer, Alois *6:* 64
Alzheimer's disease *5:* 73; *6:*
62–64
*American Ephemeris and Nautical
Almanac 4:* 172
American Red Cross *1:* 233,
235–36
American Revolution *3:* 772, 774
Ames, Bruce N. *1:* **19–23,**
19 (ill.)
Ames test *1:* 19–21
Amino acids *4:* 137, 201
Analytical engine *1:* 37, 40–42
Analytical Institutions 5: 4–5
Analytical psychology *2:* 541
Andersen, Dorothy *5:* **7–13,**
7 (ill.)
*And Keep Your Powder Dry: An
Anthropologist Looks at
America 2:* 636–37
Andreessen, Marc *5:* **14–20,**
14 (ill.)
Andrews, Thomas *2:* 655
Aneroid barometer *6:* 106,
106 (ill.)
Angiography *6:* 49, 51
Angus 1: 50
Animal conservation *4:* 92, 94,
96, 98
Animal ecology *6:* 40–42
*Animal Ecology and Evolution
6:* 43
*The Animal Kingdom, Distributed
According to Its Organization
1:* 206; *4:* 161
Animal psychology *4:* 3
Animals, ethical treatment of *2:*
411, 413
An Anthropologist on Mars 3: 830
Anthropology *4:* 66; *5:* 170,
173–74
Anthropology, forensic
5: 171, 173
Antibiotics *6:* 9
Antigens *6:* 96
Antimatter *4:* 188

Antinuclear movement
1: 124–26, 128
Antiproton *4:* 188
Apollo 11 *4:* 29
Apollo *4:* 14, 29
Apollo space program *4:* 24, 29,
30; *5:* 151, 153
Apple Computer Inc. *2:* 508,
510–11
Apple I *2:* 510
Apple II *2:* 510–11
Appleton, Edward *3:* 941–42
Archimedes *4:* 101, 106; *5:* 44
Argo-Jason system *1:* 49–50
Argonne National Laboratories
1: 290
Aristarchus of Samos *4:* 50
Aristotle *1:* 206; *4:* 101–03, 106,
160, 178; *6:* **11–16,** 11 (ill.)
Arkwright, Richard *1:* **24–29,**
24 (ill.)
Army Ballistic Missile Agency
(ABMA) *4:* 26, 28
Arp, Halton *1:* 121
Arrhenius, Svante *1:* **30–36,**
30 (ill.)
Arrhythmias *3:* 929–31
Arrow (race car) *4:* 84
Arsenic *4:* 112, 114
Arteriosclerosis *6:* 51
Articulata 4: 161
Artificial heart *2:* 502–05
Artificial intelligence *2:* 665–69;
4: 229, 230, 233; *6:* 147
Artificial radioactivity *4:* 117,
119, 122; *6:* 179
Artificial satellites *3:* 920
Asbestos *6:* 76
Asclepigenia *6:* 83
Asilomer Conference *3:* 872
Assembly line *4:* 80, 82, 85
Astatine *4:* 188
Aston, Francis *4:* 226
Astrology *6:* 28, 159
Astronomical unit *4:* 132
Astronomy *4:* 23, 48–50, 53, 56,
100, 103, 126–28, 131,
170–73, 199–202, 206–207; *5:*
82, 83, 115–18
Astrophysical Journal 1: 154

H

Homosexuality *3:* 973
Hooke, Robert *4:* 179–81, 183
Hooke's law *4:* 181
Hopper, Grace *5:* **60–64,** 60 (ill.)
Hormones *3:* 848, 853
Horowitz, Paul *1:* 72, 72 (ill.)
Horseless carriage *4:* 82, 83, 85
Hounsfield, Godfrey *2:* **483–86,**
480 (ill.)
Houssay, Bernardo A. *1:* 161
How to Know the Butterflies 1: 255
Hoyle, Fred *1:* 119, 121; *5:*
65–72, 65 (ill.); *6:* 112
HTLV-3 *6:* 70
Hubbard, Gardiner *1:* 63–64
Hubble, Edwin *2:* **487–97,** 487
(ill.), 495 (ill.); *6:* 109
Hubble Space Telescope *1:* 117,
122, 274; *2:* 493, 493 (ill.)
Huchra, John P. *2:* 381–82
Hull House *4:* 112–14
Human ecology *4:* 141
Human evolution *4:* 66, 68, 71
Human genome project *2:* 384,
387–88; *3:* 933, 937; *6:* 192
The Human Mind 2: 663
Human rights *5:* 101, 103–06
Human Use of Human Beings
3: 963
Huntington's disease *6:* 189
Huntington's Disease
Collaborative Research Group
6: 189, 190
Huntsman, Benjamin *1:* 84
Hutton, James *2:* 599, 599 (ill.)
Huxley, Aldous *3:* 885
Huxley, Julian Sorell *6:* 41, 42
Huxley, Thomas Henry *6:* 41
Huygens, Christiaan *4:* 101, 132,
181; *6:* 104
Hybridization, plant
1: 112–14, 116
Hydraulics *4:* 106
hydrodynamics *4:* 15, 16
Hydrogen bomb *2:* 686, 690;
6: 167
Hydrometer *6:* 82, 85
Hydroponics *3:* 914
Hydroscope *6:* 85
Hydrostatic balance *4:* 101

Hydrostatics *4:* 101, 106
Hydrothermal vents *1:* 51
Hyman, Libbie Henrietta *6:*
78–81, 78 (ill.)
Hypatia of Alexandria *6:* **82–86,**
82 (ill.)

I

I Am a Mathematician 3: 963
IBM *2:* 368, 511, 514
Iconoscope *3:* 1019
Id *1:* 314
Idealism *3:* 796, 798
If You Love This Planet: A Plan to
Heal the Earth 1: 129
Illinois Commission on
Occupational Diseases *4:* 113
Industrial disease *4:* 113, 114
Industrial hygiene *4:* 112,
114, 115
Industrial medicine *4:* 113–15
Industrial poisons *4:* 110,
113, 115
Industrial Poisons in the United
States 4: 115
Industrial Revolution *1:* 82, 84;
3: 946, 949, 983
Industrial Toxicology 6: 76
Infectious diseases *3:* 723, 728,
855, 858
Influenzal meningitis *6:* 7, 9, 10
Information superhighway *2:* 370
Ingram, Vernon *1:* 178
Inheritance, patterns of *2:* 651 (ill.)
Inoculation *6:* 59
Inquisition *4:* 108
Instant camera *2:* 556, 559–60
Institute of Cardiology and
Cardiovascular Surgery *6:* 47,
48, 51
Institute of Cell Biology of the
Italian National Research
Council *4:* 155
Institute of Human Virology *6:* 72
Institute for Theoretical Physics
1: 98, 100–01
Institute of Food Technologists
2: 427

National Conservation Commission *6:* 152
National Earthquake Information Center *1:* 4
National Forest Service *6:* 149–52
National Foundation for Infantile Paralysis *3:* 841
National Labor Relations Act *4:* 90
National Oceanic and Atmospheric Administration *1:* 239
National Recovery Act *4:* 90
National Space Institute *4:* 31
Natural History 2: 417
Natural History of Invertebrates 1: 208
Natural philosophy *1:* 245
Natural selection, theory of *1:* 203–04, 207; *2:* 589–90, 653; *3:* 747; *4:* 162; *5:* 121–22; *6:* 133
Nature Conservancy *6:* 45
The Nature of the Chemical Bond and the Structure of Molecules and Crystals 3: 740
Navajo (people) *1:* 58, 60
Nazis *5:* 142, 186–87
Nazism (National Socialism) *1:* 268; *2:* 461, 593
Nebulae *2:* 441–42, 444, 446
Neddermeyer, Seth *2:* 685, 687
Neon *4:* 226
Neptune *2:* 373
Nereis 2: 545
Nerve growth factor (NGF) *4:* 150, 152, 154-56
Nervous system *3:* 847–48; *4:* 151, 152
Netscape *5:* 14, 18–19
Netscape Navigator *5:* 14
Neurobiology *5:* 73
Neuroendocrinology *3:* 847–48, 851–52, 1009
Neuroendocrinology 3: 852
Neurohormones *3:* 849
Neurons *3:* 848, 852; *5:* 75
Neurosecretion *3:* 847–50, 853
Neurosurgery *4:* 33, 35
Neutrino *1:* 285, 287

Neutron stars *1:* 71, 153
New Guinea *2:* 635
The New Science 3: 764
A New System of Chemical Philosophy 1: 202
New York State Archeological Association *3:* 721
Newcomen, Thomas *3:* 947
Newlands, J. A. R. *2:* 656
Newton, Isaac *1:* 38, 41, 246, 266, 267, 267 (ill.); *2:* 435; *3:* 764; *4:* 102, 103, 128, **176–84,** 176 (ill.); *5:* 45, 166; *6:* 105
NeXT Company *2:* 513–14
Nez Percé (people) *3:* 721
Nice, Margaret Morse *6:* **136–40,** 136 (ill.)
Night vision *3:* 1022
999 (race car) *4:* 84
Nipkow, Paul *3:* 1018
Nirenberg, Marshall Warren *4:* 137
Nitroglycerin *2:* 671
Nitrous oxide *1:* 211, 213; *3:* 773
Nobel, Alfred *2:* **670–73,** 670 (ill.)
Nobel Foundation *2:* 672–73
Nobel Peace Prize *1:* 105, 109, 129; *2:* 684, 686; *3:* 738, 740, 744
Nobel Prize for chemistry *1:* 30, 33, 75, 81, 91, 96, 189, 251; *2:* 389, 474, 477, 639, 647, 654; *3:* 738, 740, 805–06, 809, 895–96
Nobel Prize for literature *3:* 802
Nobel Prize for physics *1:* 7, 13, 98, 101, 150, 153, 156, 181, 187–88, 260, 263, 285, 288; *2:* 399, 403, 607, 613; *3:* 759, 764, 787, 792, 832, 834–35, 862, 865–66, 868, 1003, 1012, 1016
Nobel Prize for physiology or medicine *1:* 161, 166, 178, 297, 302, 304, 306, 320, 325; *2:* 468, 472, 483, 486, 588, 594, 622, 627; *3:* 746, 749, 841, 843, 933, 1004, 1006, 1009, 1011

Pinchot, Gifford *6:* **149–55,** 149 (ill.)

Pincus, Gregory Godwin *5:* 30

Pio Instituto Trivulzio *5:* 5–6

Pioneer IV 4: 28

Pioneer space program *4:* 28, 201, 202

Pippa's Challenge 4: 5

Pixar Animation Studios *2:* 513–14

Planck, Max *1:* 99–100, 262; *2:* 640–41, 643; *3:* **759–65,** 759 (ill.), 813; *6:* 17, 18, 20, 178

Planck's constant *3:* 759–60, 763

Plane astrolabe *6:* 82, 83

Planetary motion *4:* 129

Planetary spheres *6:* 23, 27

Planetology *4:* 199

Plant sexuality *4:* 158

Plasma *1:* 234–35; *6:* 168, 169

Plasma physics *1:* 59; *2:* 424; *3:* 891

Plate tectonics *1:* 51; *3:* 784, 951, 957

Plato *5:* 58; *6:* 12, 16

Plotkin, Mark *3:* **766–71,** 767 (ill.)

Plucker, Julius *3:* 1020

"Plum pudding" atomic structure *4:* 224

Plutonium *4:* 188

Pneumococcus bacteria *6:* 95

Pohlflucht 3: 955–56

Poincare, Jules Henri *1:* 263; *4:* 16

Polaris 5: 151, 152

Polonium *4:* 119, 121

Polarized glass *2:* 558–59

Polarized light *2:* 557; *3:* 725

Polaroid Corporation *2:* 556, 558–59

Polio (poliomyelitis) *2:* 480–82; *3:* 815–17, 820, 838, 840–44

Polio vaccine *3:* 814, 816–18, 820, 838, 840, 842

Polonium *1:* 181, 186, 189

Polynesia, settlement of *2:* 448–50, 452

Positive reinforcement *3:* 877

Positrons *6:* 168

PowerGlove *2:* 564

Powless, David *4:* **190–93**

PPD (purified protein derivative) *3:* 856, 860–61

Pregnancy, high–risk *2:* 552

Priestley, Joseph *2:* 571; *3:* **772–75,** 772 (ill.); *5:* 180

Primate behavior *2:* 406–07, 409

Primatology *4:* 92, 94, 97

Principia Mathematica 3: 797, 800–01

"The Principles of Arithmetic, Presented by a New Method" *3:* 798

The Principles of Mathematics 3: 799, 801

Principles of Social Reconstruction 3: 800

Prison system *2:* 663

The Problems of Philosophy 3: 800

Proconsul africanus 2: 579

Progesterone *2:* 530, 532; *5:* 29–31

Project Paperclip *4:* 26

Project Phoenix *1:* 72

Prokhorov, Aleksandr *2:* 602–03

Promethean Fire 3: 977

Propositiones philosophicae 5: 2–3

Proteins *4:* 138

Protons *4:* 121; *5:* 103

Protoplasm *2:* 546–47

Psychoanalysis *1:* 308, 310, 312–14; *2:* 536, 538

Psychological Types 2: 541

Psychology *5:* 50, 52–54

Psychology of Management 5: 53

The Psychology of the Unconscious 2: 540

Psycho–neuroimmunology *3:* 853

Pterodactyl *4:* 161

Ptolemaic system *2:* 443–44, 446; *4:* 108; *6:* 157–58

Ptolemy *2:* 443; *4:* 50, 51, 54, 102, 107; *6:* **156–60,** 156 (ill.)

Public health *4:* 112, 114

Pugwash Conferences on Science and World Affairs *2:* 684

Pulsars *1:* 69, 71, 73

Punctuated equilibrium *2:* 417

Putnam, Frederick Ward *3:* 719

Pyramids *1:* 13
Pyroelectricity *1:* 183
Pythagoras *2:* 458, 458 (ill.), 460
Pythagorean theorem *2:* 460

Q

Quantum mechanics *1:* 101, 262;
   2: 680–82; *3:* 739–40; *4:* 222;
   6: 142
Quantum statistics *6:* 18
Quantum theory *1:* 99–100; *3:*
   759–60, 763–64; *6:* 17
Quarks *3:* 835; *5:* 136; *6:* 170
Quarterman, Lloyd Albert *1:* 290
Quasars *1:* 70, 117, 119–22, 121
   (ill.); *5:* 70, 105
Quasi-crystals *6:* 141, 142, 146
Quasi-Stellar Objects 1: 120
Queen of Shaba 4: 5
Quimby, Edith H. *3:* **776–79,**
   776 (ill.)

R

Ra 2: 452
Ra II 2: 452
Rabies *3:* 731; *5:* 193
Radar *1:* 7, 9; *3:* 939–41, 943
Radiata 4: 161
Radiation *1:* 125–26; *3:* 776–79,
   790, 807–09
Radiation poisoning *6:* 76
Radiation sickness *1:* 187; *2:* 688
Radio *1:* 217, 222; *2:* 614
Radioactive elements *4:* 121
Radioactive fallout *2:* 688
Radioactive tracer analysis
   4: 122, 123
Radioactive isotopes *3:* 776;
   4: 121
Radioactivity *1:* 181, 186–88;
   3: 789, 805, 807–09; *4:* 119,
   121; *6:* 179
Radioimmunoassay (RIA)
   3: 1004, 1006–09, 1011
Radiological Research Laboratory
   3: 778

Radiometer *4:* 225
Radio waves *2:* 607–08, 610–12;
   3: 893–94
Radium *1:* 181, 186, 189; *4:* 112,
   114, 118, 119
Radium Institute *4:* 118, 120, 124
Radium–D *4:* 123
Rain forests *1:* 257; *3:* 766,
   768–70
Raman, Chandrasekhar V. *1:* 151
Ramart–Lucas, Pauline *2:* 643
Randall, John T. *1:* 303
RAND Corporation *5:* 24–25
Rare earth elements *4:* 10, 12
Rayleigh, John *3:* 763
RCA (Radio Corporation of
   America) *5:* 38, 40
The Realm of the Nebulae 2: 496
Recycling *4:* 192
Redshifting *1:* 120–21, 266, 268;
   2: 381, 492
Redstone missile *4:* 22, 26, 28
Reed, Walter *6:* **161–66,**
   161 (ill.)
Reflecting telescope *4:* 176, 179
*Reflections on the Decline of
   Science in England and on
   Some of Its Causes 1:* 43
Reflex, conditioned *3:* 746,
   749–50, 752
Reflex, unconditioned *3:* 749
Reifenstein, Edward *1:* 73
Relativity, theory of *1:* 260,
   263–67, 269; *3:* 764; *5:* 140
Renewable resources *6:* 43
Repression *1:* 310, 312
Retroviruses *6:* 68, 69
Reuleaux, Franz *1:* 227
Revelle, Roger *1:* 17
*Revolution of the Heavenly
   Spheres 2:* 444
Rhenium *4:* 185-87
Rheticus, Georg *4:* 51
Rheumatic fever *4:* 210, 212;
   6: 93, 94, 96
Rheumatoid arthritis *2:* 530
Ribet, Kenneth *2:* 460
Ribosomes *4:* 137
Rice *1:* 108–10
Richer, Jean *4:* 132

T-cell growth factor *6:* 69
T cells *6:* 68, 69
Technetium *4:* 186, 188
Tektite II project *1:* 241
Telegraph *1:* 246, 248; *3:* 980, 983–85
Telephone *1:* 62, 64, 66; *3:* 982
Telepresence *1:* 49–50
Telescope *4:* 103
Telescope, reflector *2:* 442, 489; *4:* 176, 179
Television *3:* 1017, 1019, 1021; *5:* 37, 38–41
Telkes, Maria *3:* 967
Teller, Edward *2:* 399, 401–02
Telomerase *1:* 90
Template theory *5:* 73, 74–75
Tensegrity dome *1:* 336
Terbium *4:* 12
Tereshkova, Valentina *4:* **215–19,** 215 (ill.)
Tesla coil *3:* 894
Tesla, Nikola *1:* 251; *3:* **889–96,** 889 (ill.), 893 (ill.)
Testosterone *2:* 530, 532
Test tube babies *3:* 882, 884–85
Thalidomide *4:* 208, 210, 214
Thallium *4:* 225
Thenard, Louis *1:* 215
Thermodynamics *4:* 15; *5:* 97; *6:* 178
Thermodynamics and the Free Energy of Chemical Substances *5:* 96
Thermometer *4:* 102
The Theory of Games and Economic Behavior *3:* 962
The Theory of Games and Statistical Decisions *5:* 25–26
Theory of the Earth *2:* 599
This Is Biology: The Science of the Living World *5:* 124
Thomas, Vivien *3:* **897–904,** 897 (ill.); *4:* 212
Thomson, J. J. *1:* 99, 102, 102 (ill.); *3:* 806, 1021; *4:* **220–27,** 220 (ill.)
Thomson, William, Lord Kelvin *2:* 526, 611; *3:* **905–10,** 905 (ill.)
Thorium *3:* 807–08; *4:* 10

Thorium–X *3:* 808
Three Mile Island nuclear reactor *1:* 127
Throckmorton, Peter *1:* 54–55
Through a Window *2:* 411
Tides *5:* 129–30
Tiling *2:* 436
Tinbergen, Nikolaas *1:* 325; *2:* 590–91, 591 (ill.)
Tirio (people) *3:* 769
Titanic *1:* 48, 50
Tobacco mosaic virus (TMV) *1:* 306
Todd, Alexander *4:* 134
Topeka Institute for Psychoanalysis *2:* 662
Tornadoes *1:* 328–31, 329 (ill.)
Townes, Charles H. *2:* 602–04, 603 (ill.)
Townshend, Charles *3:* **911–16,** 911 (ill.)
Toy Story *2:* 513–14
Transfer ribonucleic acid (tRNA) *4:* 137, 138
Transistor *2:* 675–76; *3:* 862, 864–67; *4:* 59, 61
Trefusis–Forbes, Katherine *3:* 944
Treponema pallidum *2:* 466 (ill.)
Trieste *3:* 757, 757 (ill.)
Trounson, Alan *3:* 887
Truman, Harry S *2:* 688
Trypanosome *4:* 78
Tsao, George T. *5:* **175–78**
Tsetse flies *4:* 78
Tuberculosis *3:* 824, 855–56, 858–61
Tuck, James *2:* 687
Tull, Jethro *3:* 915
Turing, Alan *4:* **228–34,** 228 (ill.); *5:* 157
Turing machine *4:* 230, 232
The Turing Option *2:* 669
"Turing Test" *4:* 228, 233
Tuskegee Institute *1:* 146–48; *6:* 62, 63, 65 (ill.)
Two New Sciences *4:* 108
Tychonic System *4:* 128
Typhoid *6:* 161–63
Typhoid fever *4:* 113

X rays *2:* 483; *3:* 776–77, 779, 787, 789–93, 807
X–ray spectroscopy *2:* 657
X–ray telescope *1:* 45

Y

Yale School of Forestry *6:* 154
Yalow, Rosalyn Sussman *3:* **1004–11,** 1010 (ill.), 1004 (ill.)
Yang, Chen Ning *3:* 999, 1002, **1012–16,** 1012 (ill.)
Y chromosome *6:* 172, 175
The Year of the Greylag Goose *2:* 592
Yellow fever *6:* 161, 162
Yerkes Observatory (University of Chicago) *2:* 489
Young, Thomas *2:* 617

Ytterite *4:* 12
Yttria *4:* 12
Yukuna (people) *3:* 768

Z

Zero Population Growth *1:* 257
Zero–sum game *5:* 24–25
Zinjanthropus 2: 579–80
Zinn, Walter *6:* 181
Zion, Élie de *3:* 747
Zionist movement *1:* 269
Zoological Institute, University of Munich *1:* 321, 324
Zoological Philosophy 1: 208
Zooplankton *1:* 15, 17–18
Zwicky, Fritz *1:* 156
Zworykin, Vladimir *3:* **1017–22,** 1017 (ill.); *5:* 38